D0592340

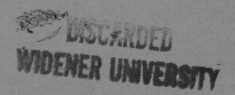

DECISIVE BATTLES OF THE BIBLE

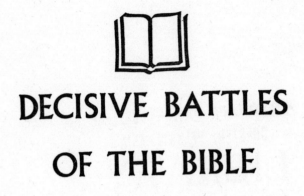

DECISIVE BATTLES

OF THE BIBLE

EDWARD LONGSTRETH

DRAWINGS BY W. T. MARS

J. B. LIPPINCOTT COMPANY

PHILADELPHIA AND NEW YORK

To Ellanor and Dent

ACKNOWLEDGMENTS

A book such as this does not spring full panoplied from any individual brow. It grows rather from the mustard seed of an original idea. Through the years many people, both laymen and clergy, have encouraged and stimulated me—and so have many books. For all of them I am humbly thankful.

One of the most useful and informative works for visualizing the topography of Palestine is the excellent *Atlas of the Bible* by L. H. Grollenberg with an introduction by W. F. Albright, Professor of Semitic Languages at Johns Hopkins University and H. H. Rowley, Professor of Hebrew Language and Literature, University of Manchester, England. I found it first in Dutch, but an English translation is now available. The Westminster *Historical Atlas of the Bible* and the Rand McNally *Bible Atlas* by Emil G. Kraeling are good visual guides to the lay of the land with commentary.

In connection with maps of these Biblical scenes: if you find two that are not in agreement, do not be disturbed. Discrepancies are not surprising considering that the tribal boundaries were fluid through the centuries and the locations of many of the ancient cities and battlefields are not known today. Educated guesses by different authorities do not always come to the same conclusion. Regarding variations in spelling the names of persons and places: some follow the Hebrew form, others the Syriac, or Greek, and still others the Roman, or the modern English, versions. To help the reader make the proper identification in difficult cases, a variant is given in parentheses.

7

Acknowledgments

Harper's Bible Dictionary is a valuable adjunct to the Bibles of the three faiths and a new book, *Adam to Daniel,* edited by Gaalyahu Cornfeld, presents archaeological material in a new arrangement beautifully illustrated to bring ancient times closer to our understanding. Of course the works of Josephus are indispensable though often confusing.

Among the books that give information about the latest historical and archaeological discoveries are: *Gods, Graves and Scholars* by N. W. Ceram, who also wrote *Secret of the Hittites; The Bible as History* by Werner Keller, *Archaeology and the Religion of Israel* by W. F. Albright, *The Geography of the Bible* by *Denis Baly, The Bible in the Making* by Geddes MacGregor, *Everyday Life in Old Testament Times* by E. W. Heaton, and *Everyday Life in New Testament Times* by A. C. Bouquet, who has also written a book entitled *Comparative Religions.*

For those who want to go more deeply into the Biblical source material, *Introduction to the Old Testament* by Herbert H. Pfeiffer may be taken as a thorough exposition. For a study of the Jewish people in the stream of time, the *Short History of the Jewish People* by Cecil Roth is especially rewarding. There are several books on the Dead Sea Scrolls and though they have little bearing on the subject matter of this book, the account of their discovery by Millar Burrows helps us appreciate the historical and ethnical background of the Jewish people. I might add that several issues of the *National Geographic Magazine* have had articles pertinent to the geography of Palestine.

Among individuals who have been helpful I am grateful especially to the staff of the Huntington Library, to Dr. Abbott Kaplan, Director of University Extension, University of California, to Frances Volts, and to Tay Hohoff, the editor who did much more than guide my errant footsteps through the English language.

CONTENTS

MAPS

following page 128

DECISIVE BATTLES OF THE BIBLE

I

THE GENESIS OF AN IDEA

THE PEACEFUL INVASION of Canaan by Abraham and Lot almost four thousand years ago began a movement that for persistency probably has no equal in human history. The first migration was actually a quiet infiltration, for the followers of Abraham and Lot occupied lands between the city-states of Canaan and kept on fairly good trading terms with them. It was not until many generations later, when Moses and Joshua led the Israelites out of Egypt in what became the second invasion of Canaan, that the invaders used armed force to seize the cities in the name of their God.

At the time of the Exodus it was not unusual for cities or tribes to band together in leagues for the purpose of preserving the worship of some deity and guarding its treasure. Such a league was usually made up of six or twelve units and is called an amphictyony, from the Greek word for neighbors.

The famous amphictyony in Greece was the league of city-states (not always the same members) that maintained and protected the worship of Apollo at Delphi and defended the treasure accumulated in that natural fortress. In Asia the most notable amphictyony was made up of twelve tribes of Israel that maintained the worship of Yahweh, Lord God of Hosts, and guarded His treasure, first in the tent of the Ark and finally in the great mountain fortress at Jerusalem.

The unique characteristic of the Israelite tribes was the nature of the God they worshipped. Their relationship with Yahweh was not a matter of mythology but was sealed by a mutual pact and founded in law and discipline.

The list of battles recounted in the Old Testament is not by any means complete. Some very important battles in Israel's history are barely mentioned or are not referred to at all. Not the battle, but the moral issues involved brought the account into the literature of the Old Testament. The interest was in the Will of God and the reason He gave them victory, or why He turned His face away from His people and inflicted on them the bitterness of defeat. For in every battle Yahweh was considered to be actively engaged either as an ally or an adversary, according to how Israel had been behaving as a people.

But win or lose, the Israelites were chosen to be His special people. This was a privilege that meant suffering as well as reward, for Israelites shared the common lot of all mankind: they were bodily mortal and they were spiritually weak. But through them, God chose to teach mankind His ways, His laws, His justice, and at times His mercy and forgiveness.

Yahweh stated His relationship with men very positively and very explicitly to Moses, saying: I am the Lord your God, you shall have no other gods before me. You shall not make for yourself any graven image of anything that is in the heavens, on the earth, or in the water. For I am a jealous God and you shall worship Me only and with all your heart and soul and mind.

That was it. There was to be no compromise, no extenuation, no equivocation. There had never before been such a concept of a God. The impact of this unique idea shook the world. It could not be exterminated. It took root in the empty places in man, possessed him, fulfilled his unfulfillment. Death and disaster only made it grow. The point all the major prophets made was that any repudiation of, or lapse from, these two basic commandments would be punished. Any backsliding generation would wish it had never been born.

In the decisive battles of ancient Israel, more was involved than the clash of arms. It was not his body the Israelite feared to have pierced, it was not his life he feared to lose; the loss he dreaded most was the loss of the favor of his God because he had broken his covenant with Him.

When at the beginning of A.D. 1948 Egypt, Syria, and the Arabs attacked Israel, it seemed as though someone had been tampering with a time clock. The belligerents and the battleground were the same as those that filled many embattled pages in the Bible.

Reading in the Bible about the ancient clashes between these same enemies, we have modern assurance that we are looking into a record that has historic value. For generations many readers had taken for granted that historical narration in the Bible was somewhat allegorical. But explorations into the past by archaeologists begun a century ago and accelerated in our generation have uncovered records that verify many of these passages.

For example, since excavations at the site of Megiddo uncovered foundations of stables that were extensive enough to accommodate hundreds of horses, the account in Judges 4 of Sisera's thousand iron chariots no longer reads like a vainglorious bit of bombast but an accurate count. The discovery of the Hittite capital at Boghaz-keui revealed the existence of a power great enough to challenge both Egypt and Assyria for control of the world, though it had completely disappeared below the surface of history. We can now understand why even David felt compelled to take devious measures to dispose of Bathsheba's husband, Uriah the Hittite.

Uncovering the official storehouses and archives of the ancient Syrians near Damascus revealed, on the seals of oil and wine jars, the cartouches of many of the kings of Syria referred to in I and II Kings, names that were long suspected of being pure inventions. And excavations on the site of Nineveh uncovered the library and records of the Assyrian kings, helping us fill in the pages of the Bible account of the long struggle between that country (in our times called first Mesopotamia and then Iraq) and Israel.

Further diggings in Mesopotamia laid bare proof of a great flood and the ruins of the Tower of Babel (Babylon). Nor have we seen the end of such discoveries, as the more recent finding of the Dead Sea Scrolls so dramatically demonstrates.

For a long time, scholars have believed that an intelligent and literary race such as the Hebrews must once have kept careful records of historical events; in fact one such record is specifically referred to in Joshua 10:13 as the Book of Jasher. It was probably from some such full historical record that the incidents of special religious significance were taken to form the inspirational books of the Old Testament.

Therefore in rereading the historical passages in the Bible it is now possible to fill out the narrative and see events in the light of our latter-day knowledge.

Each of the three great faiths has its own Bible in several editions: the Hebrew Holy Scriptures, according to the Masoretic text authorized by the Jewish Publication Society of America; the New American Catholic Edition (Douay), approved by

Cardinal Spellman; and both Protestant Bibles, the King James Authorized Version, Oxford Edition, and the Revised Standard Version, Nelson Edition; all have been used for reference in preparation of this book. Quotations, however, have for the most part been taken from the King James Version because of its supremely beautiful English. In any case, readers are urged to refer to the Bible of their choice.

To describe every skirmish and foray that occurred in Palestine during the centuries is outside the scope of this book. We choose a larger subject for a greater purpose. Moments of great decision are the important times in the history of a people, and that is what concerns us here.

By definition a decisive battle is one that decides an issue by force of arms at a time of crisis. It is caused by an accumulation of events, and results in a continuation of the advance, in a stoppage or retreat, in victory or defeat. It is the result of an aggression or of a defensive action, depending on the point of view.

But in this series of decisions there is an additional element present on the field of battle, for hovering over the struggling ranks of men is the spirit of the Lord God of Hosts, Yahweh. The decision in the Bible is ultimately His.

II

THE ANCIENT BATTLEGROUND

PALESTINE IN BIBLE TIMES did not look the way it does today
except in the general appearance of its larger earth forms. Today
it is the mere bare bones of what it once was. Its so-called wilder-
nesses were not all deserts; some were able to support life, both
of man and beast, in the way the semi-arid lands of Arizona and
New Mexico are able to graze thousands of head of cattle and
sheep in the American southwest.

A portion of America is similar geographically to ancient
Judaea. From San Diego on the Pacific Ocean eastward to the
Salton Sea the lay of the land is surprisingly like the region between Ashkelon on the Mediterranean Sea and the Dead Sea. The
American distances are greater and the altitudes higher, but both
have productive lands near the sea, then hills rising ridge on ridge
to high rocky crests beyond which, in both countries, the land
drops sharply down in arid emptiness to the edge of a salt sea
below sea level beyond whose barren shores rise the hazy heights
of another rampart of mountains.

At first glance Palestine seems a small region to have played
such an important part in the history of the world. From Dan
in the north to Beer-sheba in the south it measures only about
one hundred and fifty crow-flight miles. From the Mediterranean
Sea to the Dead Sea it is only one-third of that distance.

But on second glance, from a more comprehensive point of view, Palestine appears as a land bridge connecting two continents, Europe and Africa. On one side is the treacherous sea and on the other side the arid Arabian desert. Palestine was a corridor between Egypt on the south and on the north Syria and the world beyond.

It was a much-traveled trade route, for Egypt was one of the great ambitious powers of the ancient world. North of the Palestinian seacoast was the land of the Phoenicians, wedged between Syria and the sea with the great commercial seaports of Tyre and Sidon. North of this region was the land of the powerful Hittites and beyond that Greece. Most of the trade of the valley of the Tigris and Euphrates came not directly over the Arabian desert (though there was such a route), but followed the curve of the Euphrates northwestward, along what was called the Fertile Crescent, and so came into Damascus, the principal city of Syria.

The sea in those days was very hazardous to travelers. In winter it was stormy and almost impassable; in summer it teemed with pirates and was beset by unpredictable changes of wind. Travel by land was naturally preferred and the land route was most agreeable just at the season when the sea was most risky.

The strategic importance of Palestine is obvious.

The northern limit of the Bible country was at Dan near the headwaters of the Jordan River flowing from the slopes of Mount Hermon which is called Sion in the Old Testament. It is over nine thousand feet high and snow-covered most of the year. South of Dan were the marshes around Lake Huleh. Where the Jordan flowed through the Sea of Gennesaret or Chinnereth, later called the Sea of Galilee, the surface was already several hundred feet below sea level, and after winding through a deep and walled valley it emptied into the Dead Sea where the surface was nearly thirteen hundred feet below sea level and the mean depth of the sea almost as many feet again below the surface. On both sides of the sea the mountains rose abruptly over a thousand feet above the shores.

Nature had worked a major cataclysm here. A monstrous scar running north to south, like a gigantic trench, formed the western boundary of Palestine, giving the panorama a wild and fearsome appearance. The banks of the Jabbok River, which flowed into the Jordan from the east, were not green meadows but sheer cliffs of rock many hundreds of feet high. Cities in Judah and Benjamin no more than three air-miles apart were often separated by ravines a thousand feet deep. It was bitter terrain to use for a battlefield.

Even the strip of land through which the Jordan meandered toward the Dead Sea was in Biblical times a perilous jungle of dense thickets teeming with bears, lions, and wolves—a frightening region for people armed principally with spears and slings.

East of the Jordan and the Dead Sea there was a narrow arable plain from which the land rose almost vertically to a high tableland cut by nearly impassable gorges. These highlands were normally occupied by the Moabites and Ammonites, Arab tribes that were racially kin to the Hebrews for they were all of Semitic origin. From time to time, the Hebrews pushed eastward into this high country and occupied it, forcing the Arabs farther back into the desert.

At the southern limit of the Bible country was Beer-sheba looking out upon the bleak desert of the Negeb that was bordered by fantastic rock formations. Along the entire Mediterranean coast of the country there was not one good natural harbor.

But not all the country was so rough and inhospitable. Between the sand dunes along the seacoast and the craggy summits of the mountains were the gentle foothills of the Shephelah, the Biblical lowlands. These were fertile and hospitable. In some places they were wooded and watered by rivers and springs; there were also wells, for some of the land was under cultivation.

Groves of olive and resinous balsam trees held the soil from erod-
ing. Mount Tabor in the later time of Judges was still wooded
enough to give cover for ten thousand men. There are many passages in the Bible referring to the cutting of wood on a large
scale and even in Roman times there was wood enough near the
mountain fastness of Jerusalem to supply the needs of the Roman army for a siege.

In the middle of the Bible country, a wide fertile valley ran
east and west, dividing the land into two halves. This was the
Valley of Jezreel, later called Esdraelon by the Greeks. It was a
beautiful valley, with the hills of Galilee on the north and the
mountains of Judah on the south, the eastern end falling away
steeply down to the Jordan River. It was watered by the river
Kishon which flowed westward through a pass north of the
Carmel range and emptied into the sea. From end to end and side
to side the valley was filled with fields of grain and meadows of
grass. Here and there were a few cities that were centuries old
before Abraham saw them. The ancient cities of Megiddo,
Taanach, and Jezreel overlooked crossroads used by caravans
traveling from the Euphrates to the Nile and from Egypt to
Greece.

The slopes of the hills were colorfully tinted with the grey
groves of olive trees, the green of the vineyards, and the deeper
green of irrigated groves of balsam. In the spring of the year the
hills and valleys were splashed with the bright colors of the lilies
of the field, the anemones.

It was a land of heavy winter rains and hot summer droughts.
The rain stopped in April and did not come again until October.
The jumbled formations of the subterranean rock were so constructed that much of this rainfall was trapped underground to
supply springs and wells all the year around. In places where
water was scarce, the runoff was stored in great cisterns and underground pools for use throughout the summer.

23

The Bible country was a land of startling, dramatic contrasts and great beauty before the victorious armies swept to and fro over it, burning the cities and wantonly cutting down woods and groves. It was, when Abraham first set eyes upon it, truly a land flowing with milk and honey.

III

ABRAHAM AS WARRIOR

THE TWO MOST IMPORTANT FACTS to know about a war or a battle, are: why it was fought and what was the outcome. *How* it was fought is properly the province of military science. Naturally, the description of a conflict is often more interesting than the discussion of cause and effect, because events are described in action, but as President James A. Garfield, himself a combat veteran, plainly put it, "A war that has no ideas behind it is simply brutality."

25

As a general rule all wars begin in the pocketbook. That is to say, a people want more food, more land, more money, and so they make aggressive war; or they want to escape from burdensome taxation, or strangling import duties, or excessive tolls charged to pass through dominions straddling highways and waterways, or other forms of tribute to a sovereign power, and so they rebel; or a people must defend their land, their crops, and their industries from an attacker and so they wage defensive war.

Many arguments and ideologies are usually conjured up to conceal the basic economic situation in a confusion of words, but most wars involve economic survival of a people combined with preservation or extension of a way of life. The decisive battles of the Bible, however, involved the Lord God of Hosts and the outcome reflected His attitude toward His people.

Strictly speaking, armies do not literally *make* wars: economic pressures, ambitions and necessities, and the failure of negotiators make the wars. Peace is restored by the armed forces. But even then, again in a phrase of President Garfield's, "Battles are never the end of the war, for the dead must be buried and the cost of the conflict must be paid."

These fundamental concepts explain why the Bible so frequently tells us *why* a battle was fought and what came of it, but seldom explains *how* it was fought, unless during the action the Lord God of Hosts, Yahweh, actively intervened to effect the outcome. Among the gifts and punishments at the disposal of Yahweh were the economic rewards of prosperity and plenty for those who obeyed his commandments, or the bitter discipline of poverty and famine for those who disobeyed Him and followed false gods.

Fortunately for our understanding of these ancient times, human nature does not change. It is the one thing constant on this earth, more constant even than the hills and skies, for hills wash away, or burst apart, and stars drop out of the firmament, but in all recorded time from age to age, from race to race, and from nation to nation, human nature has not changed one jot. That is the very essence of the Divine Plan. That is why the Word of God, spoken at any time to any man, is the Word that can reach all men for all time. The constant factor of human nature in a universe of constant mutation and change is the most remarkable demonstration of God's divinity.

An account of the first decisive battle in the Bible occurs early in the Book of Genesis and concerns Abraham, son of Terah, and his nephew Lot.

Abraham came from the city of Ur in Chaldaea which was the land near the mouth of the Tigris and Euphrates rivers forming the southern part of what later was called Mesopotamia (land between the rivers), or Iraq. North of Chaldaea was Babylonia with its capital, Babylon, the central feature of which was the Tower of Babel.

The history of this region is very old, dating back to about 4500 B.C. and artifacts have been excavated indicating human habitation there more than two thousand years before that. About the year 4000 B.C., give or take a century or two, a race of people called Sumerians entered the region and settling near the mouths of the rivers called their land Sumer (Shinar in the Bible, Gen. 10:10). North of them was another people called Akkadians. These were all Semitic peoples; Nimrod the hunter, son of Cush and great-grandson of Noah, was reputed to be one of them. Their descendants became known as Babylonians, Assyrians, and Amorites.

So the time of Abraham, dating back to about 2000 B.C. was not as ancient as many people used to suppose and he came from a civilization that in many ways was very advanced. Recent excavations in Chaldaea have brought to light jewelry and appliances of almost incredible sophistication and beauty.

A day came when, with his nephew Lot and all their flocks and people, Abraham migrated southward, crossed the river Jordan,

27

and grazed his flocks and herds through the sparsely settled hills west of the Jordan as far south as Hebron. The grandfather of Israel was a nomad, a Semitic, living in a state of civilization we call the Middle Bronze Age.

In the pasture lands west of Jordan, Abraham and Lot did exceedingly well in spite of the roughness of the terrain and the numerous predatory animals that infested the woods, the deep ravines, and the hillside caves. There were towns then in ancient Canaan, city-states—Megiddo, Taanach, Shechem, Salem (later Jerusalem), Bethlehem, and Hebron—so the Aramaeans wandered into the Negeb south of Hebron with whose people they had made a treaty, and then either negotiated for watering places for their flocks, or brought the land outright in the vicinity of Rehoboth and Beer-sheba. They prospered and their flocks greatly increased. In periods of drought they even ventured as far as the pastures of northeastern Egypt during the time of the Middle Empire, which was considered by ancient Egyptians as their golden age.

There came a time when the flocks of Abraham and Lot had increased to such an extent that their shepherds were fighting one another for pasturage and water. As the Bible charmingly puts it: "And the land was not able to bear them, that they might dwell together: for their substance was great, so that they could not dwell together. And there was strife between the herdmen of Abram's cattle and the herdmen of Lot's cattle . . . And Abram said unto Lot, Let there be no strife . . . between me and thee, and between my herdmen and thy herdmen, for we be brethren. Is not the whole land before thee? Separate thyself, I pray thee, from me: if thou wilt take the left hand, then I will go to the right."

By such high diplomacy was civil war avoided. For Lot lifted up his eyes and beheld all the plain of Jordan that was well watered everywhere and so he separated from Abraham and went east. Abraham continued to dwell in the land of Canaan and Lot pitched his tents toward Sodom, southeast of the Dead Sea. This was before a great earthquake greatly changed the face of the land east of the Dead Sea, submerging cities and cutting watercourses and altering underground water tables and drainage formations.

The migration of the rich Aramean, Lot, brought him into contact with the kings of five cities, including Sodom and Gomorrah, located "in the Vale of Siddim, which is the salt sea." These five kings had been paying tribute to four kings of the Babylonian power across the desert to the east. The leader of these four eastern kings was Chedorlaomer, king of Elam (Persia or Iran), another ruled Shinar (Sumer), and the other two ruled nations also in the Mesopotamian region (Gen. 14:1–2).

The five kings of the west, thinking the four kings of the east were far away and busy with troubles of their own, decided the time was ripe to rebel against paying tribute.

But the four kings mustered their forces as quickly as they could and under the leadership of Chedorlaomer of Elam, they came across the desert and fell upon Ashteroth, east of Galilee. They then either turned south or sent a separate force directly across the Arabian desert to attack the southern region at the same time an attack was being made to the northward. At any rate, the forces of Elam fell upon the Amorites and also the Amalekites that lived between the Arabah and Egypt.

The kings of the Pentapolis assembled at the city of Zoar, which was on the flat stretch of land running out from the southeastern shore into the Dead Sea, and there in the Vale of Siddim the forces of the east and the west met. This "vale" was actually a treacherous terrain filled with slimepits, bogs, and quicksands. Out-maneuvered, the kings of Sodom and Gomorrah were routed and killed and the men of the Pentapolis fled up into the mountains.

After the looting of Sodom and Gomorrah, Chedorlaomer and his allies departed northward, taking Lot and all his goods and people captive with them.

But one of the survivors who had managed to escape from the battle found his way to Abraham, who was then living with Mamre the Amorite near Hebron, and told him the fate of his nephew.

Acting promptly, Abraham took his own three hundred and eighteen trained household servants and with his Amorite allies pursued the abductors of Lot, paralleling their march on the west side of Jordan as far as Dan, which was near the headwaters of the river.

Coming up with the encampment of the enemy, Abraham was confronted with the problem of attacking a force that must have been considerably larger than his own. He knew the men from the east were far from home and in hostile country, for they were in the midst of peoples that were paying heavy tribute. Moreover, the invaders were living off the land they were passing through then and had already passed through a short time before. Obviously the invaders were not popular and Abraham could reasonably count on the co-operation of the local inhabitants, which meant he could move with secrecy.

So, nothing daunted by the odds against him, Abraham with considerable boldness divided his own small force into two compact and easily controllable parties and in the dark of night threw himself upon his enemy in a simultaneous attack from two sides.

The surprise attack apparently put the forces of Elam and Shinar into panic for they fled in such confusion that Abraham was able to penetrate to the tents of the kings themselves and, while the enemy ran for their lives, Abraham slew Chedorlaomer and the three kings who were with him.

Then Abraham turned homeward again, loaded with booty, bringing with him Lot and his goods and all the people who had been captured. Abraham was welcomed with joy and honor not only by the new king of Sodom but also by Melchizedek, king of Salem.

When the king of Sodom asked only for the return of his people and offered all the recaptured booty to Abraham as a reward, that wise leader refused to take anything not previously belonging to him. In this way, Abraham became a great man on both sides of the Jordan, with kings for friends and plenty of water and pasturage for his huge flocks.

Because of this brave and noble behavior, the Word of the Lord came to Abraham, saying, "Fear not, Abram, I am thy shield, and thy exceeding great reward." *

* Authorized King James version, Oxford Edition. Gen. 15:1.

The Holy Scriptures, Masoretic Text of the Jewish Publication Society reads: "Fear not, Abram, I am thy shield, thy reward shall be exceeding great." Gen. 15.

The Holy Bible, translated from the Latin Vulgate, Douay Bible House, reads: "Fear not, Abram, I am thy protector, and thy reward exceeding great." Gen. 15:1.

The Revised Standard Version reads: "Fear not, Abram, I am your shield: your reward shall be very great." Gen. 15:1.

For the purposes of this book such variations are not important to the meaning.

IV

THE LONG RETREAT

ABRAHAM'S GRANDSON JACOB was a man of unusual sensibilities. Within him basic human forces continually struggled to dominate for good or evil as though he were the epitome of man. Although he was ambitious in a worldly way, yet he was also compassionate, loving, and dutiful which brought him into close communion with his God. One night he had a vision of a way to heaven, a ladder with angels ascending and descending it, at a place he named Bethel. On another occasion he wrestled with an angel victoriously at Peniel (Penuel or Phanuel) after which he was no longer called Jacob but Israel, the exact meaning of which is lost in antiquity.

Israel had twelve sons named Reuben, Simeon, Levi, Judah, Benjamin, Issachar, Zebulun, Joseph, Gad, Asher, Dan, and Naphtali. These twelve men became the leaders of tribes of Israel that bore their names except for Joseph who was later represented by his two sons, Ephraim and Manasseh, each of whom was allotted a half tribe.

The favorite son of Jacob was Joseph, sold into slavery by his brothers and taken into Egypt where he rose through sheer ability and the help of God to be second only to Pharaoh in power. This was not long after the beginning of the Hyksos dynasty, probably about 1700 B.C., but perhaps considerably later. In Joseph's lifetime many Hebrews migrated to the fertile delta of the Nile, but after his death and under another Pharaoh the Hebrews were enslaved and brutally treated.

Sometime after 1500 B.C. Moses, a Levite, was born during a time when newborn male Hebrews were under sentence of death. To save him his mother put him in a wicker basket and hid it in the rushes along the bank of the Nile near the place where Pharaoh's daughter bathed. He was discovered by the princess and adopted by her; under her protection Moses was raised and educated as a prince, learning all the wisdom, magic, and administration of a great empire.

After a series of plagues and pestilences that were blamed on the Hebrews as reprisals for their persecution, the desperate and terrified Pharaoh gave Moses permission to take his enslaved people out of Egypt. Moses lost no time. Calling together the heads of the twelve tribes he assembled them first at Rameses in the Nile delta and then quickly led them to Succoth in the Land of Goshen, which was closer to the eastern border of Egypt.

Fearing Pharaoh might change his mind when he realized so many thousands of laborers were slipping away from him, Moses moved suddenly in the night. The people left Goshen under such urgency that they did not even have time to bake their bread but had to take their unleavened dough to eat. They also took with them their flocks and herds to the number of thousands. It was a mass migration.

The route Moses took out of Egypt is debatable but it is probable that he crossed the Sea of Reeds, also called the Red Sea, at a northern marshy place south of the Bitter Lakes which are a geological extension of the sea and the site of the Suez Canal. The land there was marshy and the waterway shallow; a strong gale of well-timed wind might back up the water so that a fording could be made.

By the time the Hebrews reached this place for a crossing, Pharaoh had changed his mind and sent an army to bring them back. The army never quite caught up with them. As Pharaoh's men attempted to pursue the Israelites across the ford the wind changed and the tide surged back like a flash flood. In the swirling waters the Egyptian charioteers and horsemen were submerged and drowned. The event was certainly decisive so far as the destruction of the Egyptian army was concerned, but as a battle it was unique for the only champion fighting in the defense of Israel was the Lord God of Hosts.

The Hebrews continued their retreat from victory down the west side of the Sinai peninsula following the route used by the Egyptians to reach their copper and turquoise mines. Fearing to risk a welcome at the mines, Moses detoured eastward through the rugged mountains. Moses was no stranger to this region for he had known it before when he had taken refuge with a priest of Midian named Jethro who grazed his flocks there. The route led through the arid, bitter Wilderness of Sin and it was acutely necessary for the Lord to provide food and water for His people.

In recent times an adventuresome explorer, retracing the probable route taken by Moses and the twelve tribes, found that in season there is a great migratory flight of quail across the region (Ex. 16:13) and near that point the edible manna appears on the bushes (Ex. 16:14) while farther on there is a rocky cliff the surface of which, if struck a hard blow, will crack and scale off revealing water trickling down the face of the rock beneath the crust (Ex. 17:6).

When the Israelites reached a place called Rephidim not far from Mount Sinai they were suffering pitifully from lack of water and it was there that Moses smote the rock in the sight of all the elders and water came out of it.

While the people rested at Rephidim a leader of Arabs named Amalek came out of the desert to attack them. Moses commanded Joshua, a leader of Ephraim, to take a force of men out to give battle.

It was a desperately critical moment in the history of Israel. Only a new army recruited from former slaves stood between the rapacious enemy and the women, children, and worldly goods of the whole migration. Defeat would be complete and irretrievable disaster for all the people of Israel.

Moses took a firm hold of the rod of God, symbol of divine authority, and went up on a hill where he could watch the battle. So long as Moses stood there in the sight of the fighting Israelites with his arms upraised, Israel prevailed, but when he grew tired and dropped his arms the forces of Amalek prevailed. As the battle went on, Moses became so weary he could not hold up his arms any longer. Then Aaron and Hur, who were with him, placed a stone for him to sit on and they upheld his arms, one on either side of him, all that day until the setting of the sun. By that time, Joshua had completely defeated Amalek and held safe the people of Israel, for the Lord was with them.

When the weary people reached the vicinity of Mount Sinai they made camp and rested. But for Moses there was little time to rest. Oppressed by the responsibility for the welfare of this

35

great host and seeking inspiration he went up alone into the mountain to seek God. And on the awesome craggy summit of Sinai Moses found Yahweh.

When Moses rejoined his people he had the inspiration of a new hope. He brought down to them the Ten Commandments of the God Yahweh whose people they were (Ex. 20: 1–17) and many other laws. He told them how to construct the Tabernacle of the Lord and how to make the gold candelabra with seven branches. He gave them the symbols of Urim and Thummim and the Day of Atonement and even the law for the sect called Nazirites, the men dedicated to the service of the Lord.

Refreshed, disciplined, and reconstructed, the tribes of Israel then moved on, marching slowly northward up the east side of the Sinai peninsula through the western lands of Midian into the Wilderness of Paran. Skirting westward of the land of the Edomites they reached Kadesh-barnea where apparently they settled down for several years. Ahead of them was the Wilderness of Zin and beyond that what?

Moses needed reliable information about the terrain ahead and organized a mission to reconnoiter. He selected a leader from each of the tribes. Caleb of Judah was one. Another was Joshua, son of Nun, of the half tribe of Ephraim.

The detail pushed northward a considerable distance, passing Beer-sheba and getting as far as Hebron before they turned back. After forty days (the number forty has mystical significance and appears often in the Bible) they returned, bearing with them samples of the produce of the land to show Moses and the people —grapes, figs, and pomegranates. The land, they said, flowed with milk and honey. There was plenty of water at Hebron. They also reported that the land was occupied by strong and vigorous men who lived in great walled cities. They said the Amalekites lived in the south; Hittites, Jebusites, and Amorites lived in the mountains; and Canaanites by the sea.

Caleb was in favor of invading the country at once. The others were opposed, describing the inhabitants as giants. Some defeatists were even for turning back to Egypt as the lesser of two evils, for they had reached a point due east of their point of departure. The Lord told Moses he was provoked at the people and was inclined to punish them, but when Moses pleaded for them the Lord forgave them. Nevertheless, many did turn back at that time.

Joshua and Caleb led an army northward to try out the strength of any resistance. During the march the Amalekites and Canaanites fell upon the stragglers in the rear and destroyed them, and at a place called Hormah the expedition met such determined opposition they were forced to turn back.

The disappointment over this obstacle led to discontent and there was a rebellion against the leadership of Moses which, with God's help, was put down. When a plague struck the camp it was controlled by a fumigation with strong incense by the Levite brother of Moses, Aaron, who was the expedition's chief priest.

But the long sojourn at Kadesh-barnea marked the turning point of the migration. From this time on it was no longer a retreat but an advance, even though it was necessary at first to retrace part of the way southward in order to skirt the hostile Edomites lurking in the mountains of Seir.

On the march again, the Israelites crossed the desolate waste of the Arabah and headed north along the base of the highlands on top of which Arab peoples dwelt.

When the Israelites reached the Dead Sea their progress was completely blocked by the Land of Moab, for the Moabites occupied both the highlands to the east and the lowlands bordering the sea where once had stood Sodom and Gomorrah. Moses, while the people were climbing to the highlands, sent messengers forward to ask Sihon, king of Moab, if the Israelites could pass through his country, promising they would stay on the king's highway and not ravage fields or vineyards. King Sihon refused permission.

Realizing the Israelites actually had no choice but to advance, Sihon took the initiative and attacked them. He was defeated. So the migration pressed on and occupied all of Moab as far north as the river Arnon which was the southern boundary of Ammon, a strong and vigorous country.

By this time the Israelites had an army with a victory to its credit and high morale and they pushed northward through the lands of Ammon to Bashan which was east of the Sea of Galilee. The king of Bashan was a giant by the name of Og and he was ready to fight. The Israelites defeated him in the battle of Edrei concerning which we know nothing except that with this victory all the land east of the Dead Sea, the river Jordan, and the Sea of Galilee was conquered and open to occupation by Israel.

Although the people were disciplined and well organized, they were not yet ready to enter the Land of Canaan. Much remained to be done. For instance, at one stage of the advance Moses had called on the Midianites for help against King Og, which they had refused. Knowing he could not leave a hostile force in his rear, he sent an army of twelve thousand men which decisively defeated the Midianites and took great quantities of loot and captives.

This presented a new problem: how to divide the booty? Whatever rule was established would form a precedent. Moses decreed that one half the plunder was to go to the men who had been in the victorious army, the other half to be divided among all the other people. Of the army's share, one part in five hundred was levied for the treasury of the Lord Yahweh and of the people's share one part in fifty. This treasure was given into the care of the Levites for the use of the worship of Yahweh. The army officers came forward with a voluntary offering of gold and jewelry.

The sudden influx of so many captives prompted another measure. Moses ordered them and all who came in contact with them to be quarantined and fumigated with incense to avoid contagion.

Moses now appointed three cities in the conquered territory to be sanctuaries for anyone fleeing persecution or reprisal. One of these was Ramoth in Gilead, the name given to the heavily wooded region on both sides of the Jabbok.

It is obvious that the country east of the Dead Sea, the Jordan, and Galilee must then have been very inviting, for the tribes of Reuben and Gad and the half tribe of Manasseh asked Moses if they might take their portion there instead of waiting to reach Canaan. This was permitted them, with the proviso that they would nevertheless help the other tribes take possession of their inheritance in Canaan.

It was during this period of adjustment that the army of Israel was reorganized and the rules for exemption from military service were drawn up, with other military instructions found in Deuteronomy Chapter 20. Any man who had just built a new house and not yet dedicated it, or who had planted a vineyard and not yet eaten of it, or betrothed a wife and not yet enjoyed her, or anyone who admitted he was fearful and fainthearted, was excused from serving in the armed forces.

It had been a long and rugged march of forty years and with the reward in sight Moses knew his days were numbered. Of all the young men who were over twenty when they left Egypt, only Caleb and Joshua were still alive. Eleazar, son of Aaron, was now chief priest. Who was to be the leader of the people when Moses was gone? Another type of leadership might be needed for the hard task that lay ahead. Then at the Lord's command, Moses laid his hands on Joshua before all the people and named him his successor.

Before the sands in his glass ran out Moses named the leaders of the tribes of Israel so they would benefit from the prestige of his approval. He then publicly gave the army into the care of Joshua and the law to the Levites. And to Joshua, he said in the sight of all Israel: "Be strong and of a good courage: for thou must go with this people unto the land which the Lord hath sworn unto their fathers to give them, and thou shalt cause them to inherit it" (Deut. 31:7).

V

THE ATTACK ON JERICHO

JOSHUA'S ATTACK on Jericho was a decisive event, for whether the
Hebrews who had migrated from Egypt with Moses would enter
Canaan depended on the outcome. But it was really no battle at
all in the usual sense of the word. Beginning with what threatened
to be a long and desperate struggle, it became certainly one of the
shortest and strangest sieges on record. It is unique, too, as an
example of psychological warfare, for the ecstatic morale of the
land-hungry invaders had a literally stunning effect on the defenders.

Part of the strategy of the attack was based on the fact that the Hebrews were an exceptionally musical people. Early in the Book of Genesis, the most important divisions of the early Hebrew society are specified in order of importance: first came the owners of flocks and herds, second the musicians, and third the workers in metal. The descendants of Abraham sang and danced on any and every occasion—births, deaths, marriages, harvests, sheep-shearing, wine-making—and though they had some basic tunes, the main thing for them was the beat, the rhythm.

They had pipes and lyres for solos and song accompaniments but most of their musical instruments were percussion instruments, drums and cymbals of various kinds. Trumpets of brass and horns—literally straightened rams' horns—were used mainly for signaling. Noise was a prime requisite, not pitch. Their rams' horns could be heard even above the din of battle, the shuffling of thousands of feet of men and beasts, and the clash of arms.

World politics at the time of the attack on Jericho were in a state of flux. The exact year of the event is not known for certain but it was probably about the year 1300 B.C. The powerful Hittite Empire had ruled all of what is now Turkey, Syria, Lebanon, and Jordan, and had checked the ambitions of Egypt and Assyria; it had finally collapsed. But in the struggle to destroy the Hittites, Egypt and Assyria became so exhausted they could hardly survive their success without a long period of rest from aggressive wars in order to recoup their depleted economy.

So the sparsely settled bridge country between Asia and Africa, between the Mediterranean and the Jordan, was open to invasion by anyone pushing in from the east or west. The Canaanites of the Bible, called in history Phoenicians, perhaps because the word means Land of Purple, the color of the dye which had made them rich and famous, settled in the fertile country from the Syrian border southward almost to the border of Egypt. The Philistines, from whom Palestine gets its name, came overseas from Crete and the Aegean Islands and by force wedged themselves in between the Canaanites and Egypt, settling along the seashore.

While these migrations were going on, the Hebrew tribes that had escaped from Egyptian captivity with Moses had progressed slowly through the southern deserts of the Sinai peninsula making their laborious way northward through the rugged highlands east of the Dead Sea. At last, they were poised ready to infiltrate the tempting pastureland and wooded hills that lay invitingly open to them between the walled cities of Canaan.

But immediately blocking their path into the green pastures of the Promised Land was the river Jordan and beyond, between the river and the fertile valleys to the west, was the fortified city of Jericho. This ancient city was even then one of the oldest occupied sites in that part of the world. Although it was eight hundred and twenty-five feet below sea level it appeared, as viewed from the Jordan, to stand on a high plateau backed by towering cliffs. From a distance, it looked green and smelled fragrant for it had a good water supply and was surrounded by fields and groves of balsam under intensive cultivation.

The location was strategically important, for Jericho dominated the Jordan crossing on the direct east-west route that ran from Chaldaea on the Euphrates through the Arabian desert, crossed the King's Highway to Petra, and ended in the north-south coastal route along the Mediterranean from Sidon and Tyre to Egypt.

Jericho had a thriving commerce. The plateau it occupied was in ancient times well watered and irrigated. Its soil grew grain and vegetables, dates, figs, and grapes, balsam for incense to repel the swarming flies and sweeten the stench-laden air of cities. It grew a shrub from which an excellent durable ink was made. The products of Jericho were famous and profitable. In short, Jericho was a prize.

After wandering forty years in the wilderness under the stern discipline of the law and leadership of Moses, a new kind of challenge lay ahead of this resilient, tough people. When the Hebrew hordes left the dying Moses behind them on Mount Nebo, they had a new kind of leader for the new kind of sacrifice and trial that awaited them. The time for self-denial and elusive diplomacy was past, a time for action and violence had come. Now the whole Hebrew people, their tents, their flocks and herds, and their total possessions must be led westward to occupy a hostile land, or perish. Joshua, the man of action, was ready to lead them.

So Joshua boldly led his host of many thousands down to the banks of the river Jordan not far above where it flowed into the Dead Sea. There was no bridge at that point, no boats or barges available, and the river at flood was too deep and swift to ford with women, children, sheep, asses, and all the baggage.

Apparently it had been an unusually wet winter and the long hard rains had weakened an undercut bank of considerable height farther up the river. Undercut too far, and perhaps shaken a bit by one of the frequent temblors of that volcanic region, the cliff gave way and tons of earth and rock crashed into the Jordan, effectively damming the river. The evidence can be seen to this day.

There was no time to waste, for the river, rising fast behind its temporary dam, would soon cut a new channel through the landslide and loose a terrific torrent of water that would carry away everything in its path. Joshua ordered the people to cross immediately. The priests waded out onto the sand bars and began to supervise the crossing which was probably spearheaded by the tribe of Benjamin. The host moved forward, praising God and making haste, till the last straggler was safely over and stumbling up onto the high ground.

It was none too soon. Toward the end of the second day the Jordan tore through its obstacle and rushed down in a flash flood to the Dead Sea.

When the Canaanites heard of the providential crossing of the Israelites, "Their hearts melted, neither was there spirit in them any more," according to the chronicler of the Book of Joshua.

Turning their backs on their narrow escape and trusting in God, the people of Israel, or at least the spearhead tribes of Benjamin and Ephraim, began the slow climb up the slopes leading to the plateau that spread temptingly before Jericho. At the far end of the stretch of level land rose the ramparts of the walled city. Beyond the walls towered a great line of perpendicular cliffs hundreds of feet high, and beyond the cliffs rose in ridge on ridge the tumultuous ranges of the high desert, running like gigantic walls in a general north and south direction, cut into everywhere by dark narrow canyons as though they had been gashed by a cleaver wielded by some berserk Cyclops.

It was an awesome moment for the nomadic host as they looked up at the towering menace athwart their path, challenging their entrance into the Promised Land, for the earth appeared to be slowly writhing in resentment and poised ready to fall upon and crush them without warning.

But closer at hand on the plateau the welcome was more genial. Just ahead was a spread of green that promised supplies of food, shelter, and precious water. What though their equipment was leather and wood and stone and their mightiest beast of burden the humble ass? Had they not accepted and followed the laws of the one great God, Yahweh, Lord God of Hosts, who dwelt in the flame and smoke and thunder of fearsome Mount Sinai? They had made a covenant with Him and He with them. He was their God and they were His people. And to interpret God's will to them, they had Joshua, son of Nun.

The Bible tells us quite clearly what happened next. It is only necessary for us to understand what we are being told.

While two men were sent ahead secretly into the city to spy out the condition of the defenses, especially the condition of the walls, the Hebrews stopped part way between the Jordan and Jericho to keep the Passover. This informs us plainly enough that it was in the spring of the year, at the end of the rainy season when the wadies would be running with water, the lowlands marshy and difficult, the uplands blanketed with anemones and other lilies of the field.

During the religious festival, Joshua ordered circumcision of all those males who had been born during the forty years of wandering from Egypt through the wilderness, for none had been circumcised on the way. So the people then and there renewed their covenant with Yahweh, Lord God of Hosts, and called the place Gilgal.

While at Gilgal, the people ate up the last of their food supplies, the last of their old parched grain; from that moment forward they would have to "eat of the fruit of the land of Canaan," for the manna that had fed them from Sinai to Mount Nebo was no longer available to them west of the Jordan.

In this spirit of renewed dedication and in this plight, Joshua gave the order for all the people with all their possessions to advance upon Jericho. According to the words that begin the sixth chapter of the Book of Joshua, "Now Jericho was straitly shut up because of the children of Israel: none went out, and none came in."

In those days no leader of the Israelites took sole responsibility. It was not necessary. Yahweh was always available for advice and guidance. So Joshua conferred with Yahweh and was told explicitly what he must do—providing, of course, that he and his people were conducting themselves in such a way as to find favor in the sight of their Lord. Otherwise Yahweh would punish them for straying from His laws and commandments by administering a bitter and chastening defeat. But had they not just renewed their covenant with Him at Gilgal?

The spies Joshua had sent into Jericho returned safely, thanks to the woman Rahab who had a house on the city wall and helped them escape out a window. It was not very difficult for them to learn the true state of affairs within the city since Israelites and Canaanites, both Semitic, spoke different dialects of the same language.

Keeping their ears open in the market places, the spies had learned that the people within Jericho were afraid of the invading hosts whose God could work such wonders. They had seen also that the dimensions of the walls were formidable. The inner walls were from twelve to fifteen feet thick and from twenty-five to thirty feet high. But they had also discovered that the walls were poorly built and in many places in sad need of repair. This fact has been laid bare in recent years by archaeologists who found parts of the walls still standing to a height of eighteen feet. The stones were irregular in shape and badly fitted together, without mortar; there was much use of rubble and brick that was not fire-hardened but sun-dried like our southwestern adobe building material. The mud bricks apparently had not been washed over with a lime solution to prevent their deterioration during the rainy season, and after a wet winter we can imagine what the spies must have thought of the soft, crumbling rubble of Jericho's mud walls, however high, thick, and imposing they may have appeared from a distance.

The plan of attack was quite simple. Joshua was told by Yahweh to take all his men of war and march them around the city. The seven priests were to follow them bearing the Ark and blowing their seven trumpets of rams' horns. The host of the people were to follow after them in utter silence. This they were to do once each day for six days, but on the seventh day, the entire host was completely to encompass the city seven times. And when they had finished the seventh round, the priests were to blow on the horns and trumpets and at the sound all the people were to shout with a great shout. And it was promised them by Yahweh that when they should do this, the great walls of the city would be no further obstacle.

So this they did. Beginning each morning, the armed warriors going before the Ark and the great mass of the people following after it, they encircled the walls just beyond the reach of the slings and arrows from the battlements. The saturated ground must have been quickly churned into a soupy bog. They marched slowly, sedately, silently, for Joshua had commanded them, "Ye shall not shout, nor make any noise with your voice, neither shall any word proceed out of your mouth, until the day I bid you shout: then shall ye shout." The years of discipline and obedience under Moses were a priceless preparation. If the people had not been law-abiding and obedient to properly constituted authority, Joshua could never have carried out the divine plan.

Imagine the scene from a place of high vantage on the walls of Jericho. What a strange and perplexing sight for the defenders to look down upon. No siege machinery in evidence to hurl rocks and fire bolts, no towers or battering rams, no ladders, no hooks, no noise. Just a long, silent procession of warriors, priests, the Ark, and the great host of people. All silent except for the ghastly, hoarse, shattering blasts of the horns.

There was more to worry the defenders than this strange parade of the invading Israelites, for the encircling masses were between the city and the fields and groves. It was time for spring plowing and planting. The precious olive and balsam groves were being hacked down for fuel and the herds were being slaughtered for food. Every day of the siege brought its own kind of economic disaster and yet there was not much the inhabitants of Jericho could do to help themselves. They could not even repair the walls adequately for it was not the time of the year for sun-drying new bricks. It was altogether an anxious sight for the besieged who could not guess what the invaders were scheming to do. Cold fear and numbing despair crept into them. Their hearts grew faint.

On the seventh day, all in the Hebrew camp were up and ready before dawn. They began to encompass the city as they had done before, but now instead of one tour they continued on, around and around seven times, men, women, and children, soldiers, priests with the Ark of the Lord, and all in silence except for the hoarse honking of the horns.

After the seventh encirclement there was a pause. Then when the priests blew a strident signal with all their trumpets and horns, Joshua cried out to the people, "Shout; for the Lord hath given you the city."

So we are told the people shouted with a great shout and the walls of Jericho fell down flat, so that the people went into the city of luxury and evil and utterly destroyed every living thing— or so they said.

Perhaps we should take the complete destruction of everybody and everything in Jericho with a bit of Lot's wife, for such exaggeration was a convention in Old Testament reporting and there are many passages in the Bible in which a king boasts of taking a city, killing every living thing therein and destroying it utterly, not once but repeatedly within a few years, which surely seems a strangely redundant performance. Anyway, we are told the woman Rahab was spared, as was promised her.

Perhaps there was a timely earthquake—a frequent cause of many ruins in that region—or a collapse of the soft swampy foundation after the hard rains of winter, or perhaps the rubble-filled, mud-brick walls may have been too high to stand firm against the earth-shaking, mud-kneading trampling of thousands of feet. Or there may have been a providential intervention in some less explicable and more awe-inspiring way. We must decide for ourselves according to our own special light and insights.

49

The fact remains that recent excavations have shown that about that time the walls of Jericho were indeed thrown down and the rich, flourishing city was totally destroyed by fire.

Note: Martin Noth has recently written that probably a destruction of Jericho "had taken place before the Israelites' occupation so that the latter were able simply to take possession of the ruins and their territories," but we are concerned here only with the Bible narrative, and if more than one incident is involved, the blended account is no less valid in its purpose, impressive in its narration, and significant in its conclusion. A similar incident, though on a much smaller scale, was reported in Mayette, Kansas, on Sunday, May 17, 1959, when the spectator bleachers at a rodeo collapsed suddenly as the spectators were leaving, killing one and injuring 149. The promoter said the only way he could account for the collapse of the stands was that "the rhythmic steps of the crowd as it shuffled toward the exits may have started the structure swaying until it crumpled."

VI

JOSHUA'S CAMPAIGN AGAINST

THE AMORITES

DIRECTLY WEST of Jericho was an impassable escarpment with vertical cliffs, so Joshua had to find a way to take his people over a long detour, first north and then west to reach the high mountain ridge forming a line of communications between the Amorites and Canaanites who occupied what is now the southern part of Palestine. Guarding the nearest and best pass up to these highlands was the Canaanite city of Ai, just to the southeast of Bethel.

First Joshua sent a scouting expedition out from Jericho to reconnoiter. When they returned to report, they advised against advancing on Ai in force because of the difficult terrain. A spearhead of three thousand men was sent ahead, only to be driven back easily by the men of Ai.

Joshua rent his clothes and loudly reproached Yahweh for not letting the Israelites stay content on the other side of the Jordan, for now all Canaan would hear of their repulse, take courage and rally in great force to surround them and destroy them.

But Yahweh pointed out to Joshua that Israel had sinned by flouting His commands, for in spite of His special decree that all booty from Jericho should be dedicated to the service of Yahweh and held in safe-keeping by the priests, some of the people who had stolen and looted in Jericho had hidden part of the plunder

51

and then lied about it.

When the gold and silver and fine garments had been recovered from the guilty ones, all their other goods were confiscated into the bargain and they were stoned and burned. This restitution and purging gave the Israelites renewed confidence in Yahweh's approval of them and consequently in their own restored invincibility.

Now Yahweh revealed to Joshua the strategy by which the city of Ai might be taken. This time Joshua chose a force of thirty thousand from among his best troops and divided them. Five thousand he sent under cover of the dark of night to swing unseen around the city and hide in ravines on the far west side of Ai out of sight of the sentries on the walls but as close as they could safely get.

Then at dawn Joshua led his remaining troops, followed by all his people, up the main road to Ai. He hoped that when the men of the city saw them, they would sortie from the city walls, confident the Israelites would flee before them as the first three thousand had done. Before he got too close, Joshua led his people to the north where there was a hill separated from the city by a valley. Here on the hill he left the people. But that night, without any attempt at concealment, he led his troops down into the valley as if to prepare for a dawn attack.

The bait of all the defenseless people and their possessions encamped on the hill with only a supposedly insufficient force in position in the valley to protect them, lured the king of Ai from behind his walls. At daybreak he led his men out of the city to fall upon the Israelites. No sooner were the front ranks joined in battle than the Israelites began to fall back up the hill to the north while the people above quickly scattered in all directions into the wilderness to the northward. The Israelite army also began to scatter in detachments to protect them. The ruse succeeded not only in drawing out all the people of Ai but even the people of neighboring Bethel came in holiday spirit to join in the fun and share the loot. The city of Ai stood open and empty while its men ran about looking for Israelites.

Then Joshua gave a prearranged signal and the five thousand troops lying in ambush to the west of Ai rose up, entered the city easily and set it afire.

When the men of Ai saw smoke rising up from their city, they were amazed and confused. The Israelites also seeing the smoke rise from Ai no longer pretended to flee, but turned back and fell with savage joy upon their dismayed, scattered, and exposed enemy. The slaughter of that day reached the total of twelve thousand which included all the men of Ai and presumably many of Bethel. The king of Ai was taken prisoner, brought before Joshua, and hanged.

After that victory the spoils were divided among the soldiers inasmuch as the priests had charge of the wealth of Jericho. Then Joshua gathered the people together on the slopes of Mount Gerizim and Mount Ebal and the Ark of the Covenant was brought before the people and put down between the two mountains and after an altar had been built and sacrifices made, Joshua read to all the people the words of wisdom and the commandments of Moses.

With the way now open to the long mountain ridge that was the spine of the south, the kings of the highland cities faced a choice of being defeated one by one or of uniting against the invader. The highland people nearest Joshua were the Gibeonites and they were full of guile. Their first thought was to give battle to defend their city of Gibeon, but when they heard what had happened to Jericho and Ai, they had second thoughts and decided to try to make an alliance with Joshua.

But they were unwise enough to dissemble. They put on rags and, carrying patched waterskins and moldy crusts of bread, went on foot to see Joshua who had withdrawn to his base of operations at Gilgal.

There they exhibited worn shoes and tattered clothes, and dry, moldy bread which they said had been fresh baked from their ovens on the day of their departure, and with these deceits they made Joshua believe they had come a great distance whereas in truth they had come only an easy half-day's journey.

So Joshua, deluded, made a league of peace with them and bound it with an oath. But three days later, when Joshua had resumed his advance southward, he discovered his new allies were actually envoys from Gibeon, Chephirah, Beeroth, and Kirjath-jearim—cities which lay directly in his path through the highlands, between him and the Amorites.

The people of Israel, furious at this deception and indignant against Joshua and their leaders for being fooled by the Gibeonites, raised a loud clamor that the wily ones be put to death. But Joshua reminded them of their oath and declared they would keep it. Moreover, dead men are of little use to people on the march. Instead of killing the Gibeonites he made use of them. For punishment, they were assigned to the supply corps and from that day would be hewers of wood and drawers of water for the host of Israel. Getting rid of this hard work appeased the people of Israel and they admired Joshua the more for his constructive solution of the problem. In passing, it is worth noting that there was plenty of water and wood in the region in those days to support a considerable invading force as well as the inhabitants.

The defection of the Gibeonites worried Adoni-zedec, the Amorite king of Jebus, an ancient city on the site of the later Jerusalem, and with the kings of Hebron, Lachish, and two other cities, he decided to attack Gibeon, not merely to punish it for making peace with the invader but also to restore it as a defensive bulwark against the Israelites. When the five kings encamped before the strategic walls of Gibeon with their army, the frightened Gibeonites sent an embassy to Joshua at Gilgal reminding him of their alliance and begging him to come quickly to deliver them.

Joshua responded at once and during the night marched his whole army from Gilgal to Gibeon, coming unexpectedly upon the Amorites as they were preparing to besiege the city. Taking them completely by surprise in the early morning, he fell on them with great slaughter, threw their five divisions into confusion and pursued the remnants as they scattered.

The pursuit lasted all day in a deadly hide-and-seek among the wooded slopes and rocky ravines but as the triumphant day was drawing to a close, many of the Amorites were still alive. With the coming of darkness they would undoubtedly escape, for they were in their own country where the Israelites were strangers.

To gain time for the complete destruction of the enemy and thus harvest the full fruits of victory, Joshua needed more daylight, so in full hearing and sight of Israel he called out for the sun to stand still upon Gibeon in the highlands and the moon to stand still in the valley of Ajalon in the foothills.

The Bible is very explicit on this point: "And the sun stood still, and the moon stayed, until the people had avenged themselves upon their enemies. Is not this written in the book of Jasher? So the sun stood still in the midst of heaven, and hasted not to go down about a whole day. And there was no day like that before it or after it."

Apparently, even long ago, there were those who were skeptical about Joshua's long day and the retort in question form referring to the book of Jasher for authority was a pedantic attempt to exorcise common sense and experience. A copy of the book of Jasher has not yet been discovered. Probably it contained several items about Joshua and others, including the Song of Deborah now found in Judges 5, and was written many years after the events—not earlier, in fact, than the time of David and Solomon.

At least, we can confidently accept the concluding assurance that the sun did not stand still before or after that day at Gibeon.

The five kings were captured in a cave and hanged. Some of the Amorites, fleeing down the ravines to their foothill city of Azekah many miles southwest of Gibeon, were struck by a terrific hail storm which beat them down and killed them so that even more died, we are told, by missiles from heaven than had been slain by the sword during the day. By this it would seem the campaign was fought in late spring or early summer, and Yahweh was still on the side of Joshua.

After this victory the way was open to the south and Joshua led his people quickly from one center of resistance to another before the enemy could mobilize an effective opposition against them. His very speed was equal to an army because of the effect it had on the morale of his enemies. In rapid succession he subdued the peoples as far as Hebron and even eventually the inhabitants of Kadesh-barnea and Gaza. He moved so fast he did not turn aside to take the city of Jebus that lay out of his way.

"So Joshua smote all the country of the hills, and of the south, and of the vale, and of the springs, and all their kings; he left none remaining, but utterly destroyed all that breathed, as the Lord God of Israel commanded."

After this triumphant campaign, Joshua withdrew to winter quarters at Gilgal from where, if the worst befell, he could retreat back across the Jordan, for the principal cities of Canaan, those of the central and northern parts of the country, had not yet been taken. But enough of the country had been occupied and infiltrated to warrant advancing the center of operations of the Israelite invasion. So the Ark of the Covenant in which the spirit of Yahweh dwelt among His people, was moved from Gilgal to Shiloh, which was in the highlands north of Bethel and nearer the center of the Promised Land.

The Canaanites seemed willing to let the Israelites peacefully occupy any land they were not using themselves and entered into a careful commerce with them, though they considered them an inferior people. Apparently the Canaanites did not suspect the grand design of the Israelites, or if they did had no fear of it.

The eleven and two half-tribes of Israel formed a league to defend the Ark of the Lord and support the worship of Yahweh and protect his growing treasure. And they insinuated themselves into the unused land between Dan and Beer-sheba as best they could, each tribe relying on its own resources, to enter into the inheritance Yahweh had promised them through Moses.

VII

THE FIRST BATTLE OF ARMAGEDDON

THERE ARE CERTAIN PLACES on the earth's surface doomed by their natural features to be perpetual battlegrounds. They are the corridors giving access to regions of wealth and power. Among them is the chain of straits and seas between Byzantium (now Istanbul) and fabled Troy (known to St. Paul as Troas). Another is the English Channel. Still another is the fertile valley of the Meuse River where Caesar once fought Vercingetorix and the French fought the Germans not once but many times. One of the most ancient of the earth's contested thoroughfares is the Valley of Jezreel, later called Esdraelon by the Greeks, which we have already mentioned briefly.

Running in a northwest-southeast direction, the Valley of Jezreel cuts Palestine in half. Its western limit ends in a narrow pass in the midst of which was the chariot city of Harosheth where three thousand years ago lived Sisera, general of the armies of Canaan. At this point, the river Kishon that drains the plain flows between Mount Carmel on the south and a spur of the hills of Galilee on the north, just before it empties into the Mediterranean Sea. Here the Kishon is crossed by the north-south coastal highway from Tyre and Sidon to Egypt.

The broad, fertile plain of Jezreel narrows again at the eastern end and then drops down past ancient Beth-shan to the river Jordan and the crossing that meets the north-south royal road running from Damascus past Rabbath-Ammon (called Philadelphia in Roman times and Amman today) to Petra and the Gulf of Aqaba. At the east end of the plain, snug on a low, northwest spur of Mount Gilboa dozed the town of Jezreel with its watchtower commanding a view of the Jordan crossing far below.

About halfway between the Mediterranean and the Jordan, on high ground south of the valley, rose the double walled chariot city of Megiddo, or Armageddon as the Greeks later called it (Ar meaning hill). This Canaanite stronghold guarded a narrow defile that was a perilous shortcut southward to Hebron through the Samarian hills. Directly to the north of Megiddo was the only crossing of the river Kishon that was practical at all times of the year, for although the banks of the Kishon were dry in the summer season, they were marshy and difficult during the winter rains when the climate was cool and pleasant for traveling. The site had been occupied in the Stone Age, which in that part of the world was the period roughly from 8000 to 4500 B.C. According to archaeologists there was some sort of city there as early as 3500 B.C. The first time Megiddo enters the Old Testament record is probably during the years 1150 to 1100 B.C.

When it comes to establishing dates early in Bible history the best anyone can do is make an educated guess. The whole period of the Book of Judges amounted to something over two hundred years but the judges did not rule consecutively. Twelve are named between Joshua and Samuel, but their jurisdictions were sometimes relatively local and their lives often overlapped. Compiling a sequence that adds up to a total which will check out accurately with events before and after is not possible with the sketchy data we have available at present.

After Joshua had gone to Abraham's bosom, the Israelites enjoyed some success in moving into their inheritance in the Land of Canaan. Judah took Gaza and Askelon and the seacoast defended by those cities, and pushed south beyond Hebron, but other tribes were less fortunate. The tribe of Benjamin failed to take the city of the Jebusites (later Jerusalem). Manasseh was unable to take Beth-shan, Taanach, or Megiddo, and in the north Asher could not drive out the inhabitants of Accho (Acre) nor Naphtali the people of Beth-shemesh. They were, however, by occupying the land all around the cities, able to put some of the inhabitants under tribute, and to a considerable extent coexisted comfortably with the Canaanites.

But the Lord did not approve of this arrangement His people had made with the enemy because the Israelites began to show more than a little interest in the Canaanite worship of Baal, and a new generation arose "which knew not the Lord, nor yet the works which he had done for Israel."

"And the anger of the Lord was hot against Israel." The result was that the Israelites soon lost their advantage and instead of collecting tribute from the Canaanite cities were themselves paying tribute until their condition became not much better than slavery.

For a period of forty years their lot improved somewhat but again the people lost favor with the Lord and they were successfully attacked by Moabites, Ammonites, and Amalekites.

Later Moab was reconquered and the land had rest "for four-score years." It was during this period the Israelites instituted a rule by judges, men especially wise in experience and sound in judgment who were designated to settle disputes among the people.

One of these judges was a woman who lived more than a thousand years before Christ. Her name was Deborah and she sat under her palm tree between Ramah and Bethel in the hill country of Ephraim and judged her people. She was a most remarkable personality and in all the pages of the Bible we do not find her like again. Deborah was the wife of Lapidoth and a mother in Israel and it went to her heart to see the misery of her people under the commercial yoke of King Jabin of Hazor and the Canaanites who had been oppressing the Israelites intolerably for twenty years. The only effective armed force available to Deborah among the north-central tribes numbered a scant ten thousand scattered among the hills under the command of Barak of Kedesh in Naphtali. Barak had been a prisoner of the Canaanites and knew something about them at first hand.

Until recently most readers thought the Bible fancifully exaggerated the account of Sisera's nine hundred iron chariots but excavations on the site of Megiddo have uncovered the stone foundations of stables with stalls and stone cribs for hundreds of horses.

The Canaanite chariots were not made entirely of iron but were braced and reinforced with iron and had wheels with iron tires. This made them a deadly weapon, for the Canaanites could drive home their chariot charge easily and effectively on rough dry ground that would shatter ordinary wooden wheels. The Israelite infantry would be mowed down like hay by such a devastating offensive weapon.

Faced with the apparently insuperable dilemma of defeating the iron chariots with infantry, Barak despairingly watched the fighting spirit and stamina of the inactive Israelite warriors deteriorate year by year while Deborah sat patiently under her palm tree judging according to the laws of Yahweh and Moses. The men with battle experience were growing old and the young men were passively resigned to their lot as a subjugated people. Time was running out for Deborah and Barak.

Then the redoubtable Deborah had an inspiration direct from Yahweh. She summoned Barak to her tree and announced to him that the Lord God of Hosts had commanded her to strike the Canaanites and free His people. It was useless for Barak to point out that he had but ten thousand foot soldiers to match the harnessed might of Sisera. God had spoken and Deborah had clearly heard Him.

In His name she commanded Barak to assemble the men of Naphtali and the neighboring tribes of Zebulun and Issachar and any of the other tribes of the amphictyony that could be persuaded to send levies.

Barak rather sarcastically inquired where they could assemble such a host without being discovered, attacked, and cut up piecemeal by the watchful and alert enemy.

"Assemble them on the slopes of Mount Tabor," Deborah directed.

"If you will go with me, then I will go," Barak said. "But if you will not go with me, then I will not go."

"I will surely go with you," Deborah answered firmly.

Mount Tabor was the logical place for assembly for not only was it at the juncture of the lands of Naphtali, Zebulun, and Issachar, but it was on the north side of the Valley of Jezreel some distance northeast of Megiddo and at that time was heavily wooded so that the number of the troops would be hidden from the far side of the valley; the timbered slopes would be quite safe from any charge by the heavy chariots of Canaan. Moreover the

Kishon flowed between Tabor and Megiddo.

Barak reminded Deborah that it was not the right time of year for a campaign. It was still early in spring and the rainy season had not yet passed. And since the Bible has given us a dramatic clue between Deborah and Barak in dialogue, we might imagine a continuation of it describing the narration.

"So much the better," said Deborah. "Pray for rain."

So the Israelite soldiers from the tribes of Ephraim, Benjamin, Manasseh in the west, Zebulun, Naphtali, and Issachar assembled on Mount Tabor and waited for Deborah to reveal Yahweh's commands. At last, one day great thunderheads piled up in the sky to the northeast, masking in black menace the snowy slopes of Mount Hermon. A cold wind bore the smell of rain. The hour had come.

At a word from Deborah, Barak led his infantry out of wooded Tabor down onto the plain at the head of the valley and crossed over to the south bank of the swollen Kishon. The Canaanites could hardly believe their senses—which was the only thing they did believe in—but there in full view, advancing toward Megiddo, was the host of Israel on foot.

Astonished and contemptuous, the Canaanites opened the gates of Megiddo and the iron-shod chariots, each with a driver, a spearman, and a shield bearer, and drawn by a pair of spirited horses, poured out through the double walls and down the ramp onto the plain.

Barak in dismay pointed from them to the increasing fury of the storm driving down upon them from the northeast.

"But the storm is at our backs and full in the faces of the Canaanites," Deborah explained.

The wind-driven rain brought with it the nagging sting of sleet. The river Kishon, already full, began to overflow its low banks as the chariots formed ranks before Megiddo.

"Now!" exulted Deborah, "the Lord God of Hosts is with us.

Attack! Straight down the river for the walls of **Megiddo**."

Barak and the Israelites, trusting in their God, moved forward resolutely.

The Canaanites did not wait for them but charged, confident they would cut the foot soldiers to pieces.

But now flash floods poured down from the mountains onto the saturated ground of the valley, turning the central part into a great lake of mud. As the two hostile lines came closer, the heavy chariots, one by one, slowed down, mired in the soupy ground, bogged down, stopped.

The fiercely inspired infantry of Israel ran forward into the midst of the sinking chariots and floundering, frantic horses, and cut down the struggling Canaanites.

When the day was over and the storm had blown itself out, the army of Canaan was no more. The victorious men of Israel pursued the last survivors of the forces of King Jabin into the hills and proud Sisera himself, slinking furtively into the night, was murdered by Jael, widow of Heber the Kenite. The Kenites, reputed to be the descendants of Cain (one of them was a father-in-law of Moses), were famous as the iron masters of the south and were associated from time to time with the Midianites and Amalekites. Heber was lost in the battle, probably driving one of the chariots he had helped to make.

Part of the story of Deborah is told in Judges 4, the rest of it in Judges 5 called the Song of Deborah, which is one of the oldest and certainly one of the most touching and beautiful passages in the Bible.

So after many years the children of Israel were free again and the fertile grasslands and grain fields of Jezreel were open to them. Throwing off the yoke of Canaan they took control of the great crossroads of commerce, the trade routes from Greece to Egypt and from Tyre and Accho to Gilead that crossed before the smoking ruins of Megiddo. "And the land had rest forty years."

Under her palm tree Deborah sat again to judge her freed and prosperous people, while the mother of Sisera waited in vain at her latticed window for a charioteer who would never return.

VIII

GIDEON AND THE CAMELS

THE FORTY PEACEFUL YEARS Deborah and Barak had brought to
Israel came to a sudden end. The Israelites were driven out of
their tents and forced to hide among the boulders in remote
wilderness ravines, or cower in caves high on steep mountain
sides. At the same time, the Canaanites and Philistines were
penned up in their starving cities.

The menace came from regions far to the southeast across the
Jordan from the land of Midian which today we call Arabia and
Saudi-Arabia. The Midianites then, as now, were a branch of the
Semitic race. Allied with them were the marauding nomads called

66

Amalekites because they were descended from Esau's grandson Amalek. These rascals roved the desert south of Canaan between Midian and Egypt.

The Midianites had tamed the wild camel and used these unpleasant beasts for transportation probably early in the second millennium B.C. It was to a camel caravan of Midianites on their way to Egypt that the sons of Jacob sold their brother Joseph long before Moses was born. The camel's ability to go great distances through the desert without food or water and at a considerable speed, as speed was then reckoned, made it a weapon of great effectiveness against a people tied down to the pace and range of the ass.

Since the Midianites were not a provident people, but wasteful and predatory, they often had to look outside their own borders for food and consequently eked out a living by raiding their neighbors. The use of the camel greatly extended the range of their striking power and one year before the millennium B.C. at harvest time in Canaan they dashed through the land of Moab, took their camels across the shallow fords of autumnal Jordan and, taking the Israelites and Canaanites completely by surprise, struck with overwhelming ferocity.

Like an all-consuming plague of locusts, they penetrated even as far as Gaza in the land of the Philistines. When they withdrew to their own land of Midian as quickly as they had come, they left behind them a land stripped of everything that was edible, even trees, vines and shrubs, for like all backward and ignorant people, they destroyed what they themselves could not use, or understand.

The natives who had escaped the scourge and had taken what they could into hiding, now emerged to recover their land and face starvation, for the Midianites had driven off all the asses, sheep, and oxen. As the time for the next harvest approached, the people of Palestine—whether they were Philistines, Canaanites, or Israelites—lived in daily terror.

67

There were some years when the Midianites did not appear, but more frequently they did. Such catastrophes the Israelites attributed to the punishing hand of Yahweh who was displeased because so many of them had shown fear and appeasement toward Baal, the god of the Amorites, and Yahweh was a jealous God. So the people of Israel repented and prayed to Yahweh to deliver them from the Midianites.

It is small wonder the Israelites believed that the strategy and tactics used in their decisive battles for survival were directly inspired by their God Yahweh, for each crisis was without precedent in their own experience, yet was met by their leaders with bold confidence and handled with imagination and inventive improvisation. Moreover, each man who rose to lead them in their hour of desperation seemed to appear from the most unexpected source and in the most inexplicable manner.

The man Yahweh chose to deliver the people of Israel from the scourge of the Midianites and their allies the Amalekites, was Gideon, son of Joash the Abiezrite, who lived in a town called Ophrah in a border region in the allotment of Manasseh.

One day when Gideon was threshing his grain secretly near his wine press so Midianite spies might not suspect what he was up to, an angel of the Lord appeared and announced to Gideon his God-given mission to rise up and save his people. After some impressive ceremonies, Gideon accepted; there on the spot he built an altar dedicated to Yahweh and during that very night destroyed the altar and sacred grove of Baal. But while the fathers of Ophrah were considering what to do with Gideon for such a bold action, the Midianites suddenly appeared and camped in the fertile Valley of Jezreel.

In the middle of the valley was a hill called Moreh, a spur of Mount Tabor on the north side of the valley near Jezreel. Gideon's followers pitched their camp opposite it by the well of Harod on the northwest side of Mount Gilboa.

Now the desperate Israelites that were assembled to confront the fierce Midianites were very many, and the Lord told Gideon they were too many because if they won a victory they might think it was all their own doing and credit the Lord Yahweh with no part in it. So Gideon was directed to tell the people that all those who were afraid to face the enemy could depart and return home. Twenty thousand left the field. The ten thousand who remained were more than enough, no doubt, to keep fed and under control.

It still seemed to the Lord there were too many for the plan he had in mind, so he directed Gideon to bring them down to the water to drink and to watch how they drank. All those who kneeled down and lapped up the water with their tongues Gideon was to send away. Those who took water into their hands and drank in that way were to be kept to confront the Midianites and of these self-disciplined men there were no more than three hundred in all that host. But only these the Lord God of Hosts was willing to have serve as His weapon against the Midianites and Amalekites who were encamped "along in the valley like grasshoppers for multitude; and their camels were without number, as the sand by the sea for multitude." And the little army with Gideon was not afraid because Yahweh was with them.

A force of only three hundred picked men was easy to control. Gideon divided them into three companies and to each man he gave a trumpet and also an empty earthen pitcher with a lamp inside. Gideon himself led one group, directing the other two to take signals from him and do exactly as he did. Then they all crept down as close to the tents of the enemy as they dared, taking care to make no sound.

At the beginning of the middle watch of the night when the new guards of the enemy had just been set, Gideon blew his trumpet, broke his pitcher and with his left hand held high the lamp. All three hundred men immediately did the same thing, so that the valley suddenly echoed with the noise of blaring trumpets and crashing pottery. Lights now appeared everywhere on the slopes above and around the tents of the enemy in the valley. Then Gideon and all his men with a great shout cried, "The sword of the Lord and of Gideon."

In the hush of the night the sudden uproar raised a thousand echoes. The din was terrifying. Pandemonium and blind panic possessed the Midianites and Amalekites who sprang up out of sound sleep and in the dark fell upon one another with their swords. The great herds of camels, never the best-tempered creatures at any time, stampeded in all directions, trampling their hysterical masters under foot. The multitude of the enemy ran screaming through the night, they knew not where nor from what.

Quickly Gideon sent word to the people of Naphtali and Manasseh and even Asher to come with him and pursue the Midianites. All the men of Ephraim gathered together and, following Gideon across the Jordan, captured the two Midianite princes Oreb and Zeeb and killed them.

"Thus was Midian subdued before the children of Israel, so that they lifted up their heads no more. And the country was in quietness forty years in the days of Gideon." The people offered to make Gideon king of all Israel, but he declined and went back to his farm at Ophrah.

IX

COMBAT IN THE VALLEY OF ELAH

GIDEON'S SON ABIMELECH was a bloody man who murdered all his brothers, and his judgeship was turbulent. He felt that the men of the city of Shechem dealt treacherously with him. Shechem was one of the oldest cities of Canaan; strategically important, it commanded the narrow east-west pass between Mount Ebal and Mount Gerizim, on the border between the lands of Ephraim and Manasseh. Abimelech divided his forces into three companies, disposing them in the fields outside the city to make an ambush for the inhabitants when they came out to work. He fell upon them according to plan and after a battle lasting all day he took the city and killed all the people and then, after leveling it, he "sowed it with salt."

The eighth of the twelve judges was Jephtha and there is a discrepancy in the Biblical account of his parentage. The J source (the narrative of the southern tribes) says he was the son of a Gileadite, "a mighty man of valor," and a harlot, and that he led the life of an outlaw; but the E source (the narrative of the northern tribes) describes him as an established householder and family man. Whichever is true, he was an important and respected leader for the men of Gilead east of the Jordan chose him to be their king and help them against the men of Ammon, who lived on their southern border and whose capital city was Rabbath-Ammon. The leaders of Ammon rejected the peace proposals offered them by Jephtha, whereupon he made a rash vow to the Lord that if he won a victory against the Ammonites he would sacrifice as a burnt offering whatever came out of the doors of his house to welcome him on his triumphant return. The first creature to come out to welcome him was his daughter, his only child. The distracted father granted his daughter's request that for two months she and her maidens could go up and down the mountains "bewailing her virginity" after which he did as he vowed he would do and sacrificed her to Yahweh.

During the period of the judges many of the people lived in tents in order to be near their flocks and were still in the cultural status of the Bronze Age. Their armor was made of wood and toughened leather, in rare cases augmented by a breastplate and helmet of brass. Their weapons were the spear, bow and arrow, and throwing stick. They had short knives of bronze but most of the sharp edges they used were made of flint. Even their sickles for harvesting grain were wooden pieces with many small flints set along the edge. The only iron they owned was meteorite iron which was more precious to them than gold and worn only for ornament.

As the southern tribes pressed south in an effort to occupy their inheritances, they came into contact with the Philistines, a race of people that had come over the sea from the west and settled along the coast between Canaan and Egypt. The Philistines had, like the Canaanites, already entered the Iron Age and jealously guarded their secret of smelting iron and forging it.

As the people of Dan and Judah moved their flocks along the highlands, they were irresistibly tempted to push down the more verdant western slopes until they came into contact with the Philistines below. They could trade their wool and hides and mutton with their arrogant neighbors and take in exchange iron blades for their spears and pruning hooks and iron points for their ploughshares.

But the Israelites were obliged to go to the Philistines humbly and at exorbitant cost to get their iron points sharpened and repaired. This did not lead to the development of cordial relations between them. There was continual pushing to and fro along the border east of Gaza and Ashkelon and Joppa. They took turns at aggression, for an increasing population put great pressure on Israel to expand. But with deserts to the south and east of them and Israelites north of them, the people of Judah and the south could only move westward. This the Philistines were determined to prevent and opposed with literally a wall of iron, for the Philistine warrior went into battle preceded by a shield bearer who lugged a great iron shield behind which the Philistine fighting man stood to throw his spears and await the onslaught.

In combat between large armed forces, what could the sons of Israel accomplish with their inferior arms and armament against an enemy shielded by iron and armed with steel? Their only strategy was to lie in ambush in the fields of ripe grain and spring upon enemy detachments, trying to overwhelm them by surprise and local weight of numbers, guerrilla fashion.

This style of warfare was perfectly suited to the temperament and abilities of the next-to-last judge and the most colorful of them all after Gideon, the hero Samson. He was a member of the tribe of Dan which had settled in the foothills between the mountains of Benjamin and the seacoast cities of the Philistines. Samson came to leadership probably about 1050 B.C. He led no great armies and won no decisive battles but with his inventive and resourceful guerrilla tactics he was exactly the kind of leader Israel needed to keep the Philistines at a distance and put heart into the children of Israel.

After the death of Samson the Israelites were desperately in need of a new leader and the Lord gave them the prophet Samuel, an Ephraimite. His mother Hannah had been for a long time childless but after prayers and a pilgrimage to the Ark of the Covenant, which was still at Shiloh where Joshua had left it, and vowing her first born son would be dedicated to the service of Yahweh, she bore Samuel.

The site of Shiloh has been discovered in modern times in the highlands of Ephraim on the road north from Jerusalem at a point about nine miles north of Bethel.

The Ark was made of acacia wood, called in the Bible shittim. As described in Exodus (Ex. 25:10–22) it was something less than four feet long. Its breadth and height were proportionally smaller and of equal measure. It was overlaid with gold inside and out and equipped with two rings on each side and two poles to fit through the rings for carrying it. Inside the Ark were probably kept the stone tablets of the law, the covenant made with Yahweh by Moses at Sinai. Above the lid of the Ark was the Mercy Seat, also of gold with two gold cherubim, their wings outstretched, hovering over it and looking down upon it.

The Philistines, also under population pressure to find additional lands, took the offensive against Israel and it was Samuel's hard task to stop, if he could, the aggressive advance of the enemy. In this the Ark of the Lord itself won a specific and individual victory over Dagon, the god of the Philistines.

The Philistines were encamped at Aphek (later called Antipatris) a city in the plain over twenty miles west of Shiloh and only a few miles from the Mediterranean Sea. The Israelites pitched at Ebenezer, the site of which is not known today. In the battle that ensued, the Israelites were defeated with a loss of four thousand men.

The prospects for the Israelites looked so hopeless and their morale was so low, that the elders of the people thought it might hearten the men if they could see the Ark of the Lord and they sent to have it fetched out of Shiloh. When the Israelites saw the Ark being carried into their camp their heads went up, their eyes brightened, and their sense of destiny surged back into their hearts. They gave a loud shout "so that the earth rang again." They made such a joyful uproar the Philistines heard it and when they found out the reason for it they became anxious.

But the Philistines had no intention of becoming slaves of the Israelites whom they looked down upon as an inferior people and they again decisively attacked the Israelites. The children of Israel fled leaving thirty thousand dead on the battlefield. And the Ark of the Lord was taken by the Philistines and carried to Ashdod near the sea north of Ashkelon and there they put it down in the house of Dagon, their god. And one of the daughters of Israel, the wife of Phinehas, led the lament, "The glory is departed from Israel: for the Ark of God is taken."

A very peculiar thing happened during the first night the Ark rested in the temple of Dagon, for the next morning the priests of Dagon found their idol had fallen on its face before the Ark of the Lord and though they set it up again, by the following morning its head and hands had been cut off; "only the stump of Dagon was left to him."

In fear the people of Ashdod sent the Ark to Ekron, but the

people of Ekron were also afraid to keep it. None of the Philistine cities wanted to risk disaster or be victimized by the power of the Ark and after seven months of bickering they decided to return it to the Israelites. Building a new cart to do it honor and putting beside it a peace offering of gold, they delivered it to the men of Beth-shemesh which was located several miles east of Ashdod. It was then forwarded to the inhabitants of Kirjath-jearim, a city on the border of Dan and Benjamin near Judah.

"And the men of Kirjath-jearim came, and fetched up the Ark of the Lord, and brought it into the house of Abinadad in the hill, and sanctified Eleazar his son to keep the Ark of the Lord" (I Sam. 7:1).

For a few years thereafter Samuel judged the people of Israel in peace from his home at Ramah in Ephraim, an easy day's journey southwest of Shiloh. Unfortunately "his sons walked not in his ways, but turned aside after lucre, and took bribes, and perverted judgment." The people in their discontent asked Samuel to give them a king and with God's help he chose for them a wealthy and devout member of the tribe of Benjamin named Saul and anointed him first king of Israel about the year 1000 B.C.

Saul established his capital at Gibeah, three miles north of the site of Jerusalem and established his leadership over the tribes by fighting all their enemies. During his brief reign he welded the tribes of Judah and Benjamin into an effective fighting force and, under pressure from the people to lead them down into the grassy lowlands, he decided to risk a decision with the Philistines in battle. His army did not progress far before its way was blocked. On a slope along the west side of the Valley of Elah, the Philistines drew up their well-armed, formidable forces and the descendants of Judah kept a discreet distance away on the eastern side of the valley.

There, day after day, the great champion of the Philistines, an oversized brute named Goliath, strode down into the valley and dared any man among the Israelites to come out and fight him—winner to take all.

"Choose a man for you," roared Goliath, "and let him come down to me. If he be able to fight with me and to kill me, then will we be your slaves; but if I prevail against him and kill him, then you shall be our slaves and serve us."

This galling challenge was repeated daily for forty days. The invitation to commit suicide did not appeal to any among the hosts of Judah from commander Abner to the lowliest soldier. And meanwhile King Saul sat brooding in his capital at Gibeah nearly twenty miles from the shameful scene.

At this critical juncture, Jesse, an owner of considerable flocks near Bethlehem, began to grow anxious about his three sons who had gone down toward the Valley of Elah, which was only a few miles west of Bethlehem, to serve in the army of Judah under Abner. Calling his youngest son David from his flocks, Jesse gave him a large supply of cheeses, bread, and parched grain and sent him to give the food to his brothers and their commanding officer and bring back news of them to their anxious families.

The youthful David set out with no other weapons than his sturdy staff and a sling with a pouch of carefully chosen smooth round stones about half the size of his fist.

David was a poet and something of a dreamer, which is to say he was a man of vision and imagination and some ingenuity. When he saw the bragging Goliath stride down into the valley covered in flashing brass with a great tempered steel blade in his hand and a servant bearing a huge iron shield before him, he saw what every other son of Judah saw. But David saw something more. He saw the bearded, ruddy expanse of the giant's big face quite exposed and entirely unprotected. David also perceived that he could with perfect safety get almost within a spear's throw of that big face.

While watching his flocks alone on the wild hills of Judah, David had been armed with nothing more lethal than his club, his sling, and the co-ordinated strength of his lithe young body, yet he had more than once single-handed killed bears and lions that attacked his flock. Long, patient practice had made David deadly with his sling and confident of his aim.

Each time David heard the loud-mouthed Goliath defy and mock the army of the only true living God, he became more indignant and more filled with the spirit to champion his God. Moreover, he had heard that a rich reward, including marriage with the king's daughter, was offered to any Israelite who would kill Goliath. With these incentives, David decided to risk his strength against the champion of the Philistines.

His brothers were angry when they heard him make the mere suggestion and Abner could hardly be blamed for refusing permission. But David was confident and persistent, so to get rid of him Abner sent him to King Saul—a rare example of "passing the buck" upward.

David had once been harpist to the gloomy Saul and went before him unabashed to explain his plan, carefully documenting all his claims to prowess and marksmanship against the wild beasts. At last, in his desperation, Saul decided to risk the outcome and, giving him permission, at the same time offered David his armor which was the best available in Judah.

Even so, it was not proof against the steel-armed strength of Goliath's right arm and David was shrewd enough to know it. One blow of Goliath's sword would slice through the fragile shield and split the brass helmet and the head within it. In any case, David was unaccustomed to moving in cumbersome, heavy armor and it had no part in his plan. He had no intention of coming within reach of Goliath's sword arm.

Yet in refusing the armor, David was tactful. He had not proved himself worthy to wear it, he said. He must first prove himself in combat before he could accept such an honor.

So he took back with him into the Valley of Elah only his staff, his sling, and five specially selected uniform round stones from the brook.

As the handsome and apparently quite unarmed youth strode down into the valley to confront the champion of the Philistines, Goliath roared with indignation.

"Am I a dog," he bellowed, "that you come at me with a stick?"

David was no less inventive. He replied that he would make his loud adversary into a carcass for the birds and beasts to feed upon and that with Goliath's own sword he would cut off his head and therefore he had no need of one of his own.

They shouted insults and defiance at one another until at last, goaded by the taunts of the insolent stripling, Goliath came forward intent on splattering the blood and brains of the brash youth upon the ground. David ran a little way to meet him. When close enough, but before he entered the range of Goliath's armament, David stopped short, took a stone from his pouch, put it into his sling, and with a flash of practiced, co-ordinated skill whipped the sling around and let the stone fly. The stone went straight to its mark in the middle of the exposed Philistine brow and crushed in the bone. The giant fell prone upon the ground. David ran forward and, standing on the fallen body, cut off Goliath's blasphemous head.

At this sight the Philistines were dismayed. They turned and fled, pursued by the sons of Judah.

One outcome of this combat, frequently overlooked by the casual reader, was that the Israelite warrior who possessed the forged steel sword of Goliath could be leader of Judah. By right of conquest the sword and armor of Goliath now belonged to young David, but as a precaution against civil war and to maintain the peace in Judah, the prophet Samuel wisely took Goliath's armor to his sanctuary at Ramah. There he held it in safekeeping until David, fleeing for his life from the jealous hatred of Saul, later claimed it for his own defense.

X

THE PHILISTINE CONCLUSION

THE PROMISE MADE by Goliath to the warriors of Judah was not fulfilled. The Philistines had no intention of allowing the Israelites to frustrate their determination to move inland from their sea-coast cities. As they increased pressure on the western borders of Judah it became easier for the Benjaminite King Saul to unite the exceedingly independent peoples of Judah in order to resist.

But in spite of an elite guard organized around the young warriors David, Abner, and the king's son, Jonathan, King Saul was not able to stand against the Philistines. The sacred city of Shiloh was taken and utterly destroyed.

Though his plight was already serious enough, Saul became so furiously jealous of David's military exploits—he could not bear to hear the handmaidens singing "Saul hath slain his thousands, and David his ten thousands"—that David had to fly for his life into the mountain wilderness of Judah. There many hardy warriors soon sought him out to enlist under his guerrilla leadership, and knowing he could not hold out there against Saul without a fight, he led them as mercenaries into the service of the Philistines. His former enemies welcomed him gladly and when David asked for a place to dwell, the king of Gath gave into his safe-keeping the fortified city of Ziklag which was perhaps a dozen miles north of Beer-sheba.

The Philistines now decided to avoid a direct frontal attack on the strong high mountain positions of Judah and detoured to the north, intending to cut eastward through the fertile land of Benjamin to Jericho and the Jordan, thus isolating Jebus (Jerusalem) and the country along the mountain ridges south of it from the rest of Israel. They had superior equipment and manpower and did not expect any serious opposition.

As they advanced, Saul withdrew before them as far as Gilgal. Unable to support a large army there, he sent many of his followers back to their homes, keeping with him only the most valiant and reliable.

The Philistines easily took Michmash, which was nineteen hundred feet above sea level and commanded a deep strategic pass leading down to the Jordan. This gorge was only a few miles north of Saul's capital city, Gibeah in Benjamin, which was itself about half way between Michmash and Jebus. Garrisoning the city of Michmash, the Philistine army camped in the pass and sent raiding parties in every direction to despoil the country round about.

A serious military and economic consequence of the war between Saul and the Philistines was that the men of Judah and Benjamin could no longer get iron or have their tools sharpened or repaired, for the Philistines had allowed no smith to operate outside Philistia and although a few Israelites may already have learned something about iron manufacture they were shut off from a supply of raw material. The people of Michmash and the exposed countryside had no choice but to join the Philistines, at least in appearance, and many of them actually moved into the Philistine camp to do most of the menial labor.

As the situation worsened, Saul managed to interpose himself and an army between Michmash and Gibeah in an effort to protect his capital, but he was impotent to save his people from the disastrous raids and forays of the Philistines who were, of course, living off the country they occupied. The best Saul could do was to advance to the southern rim of the gorge and gaze down in frustration at the Philistine army smugly encamped in full view below.

Then one day, Saul's son Jonathan, tired of the ruinous stalemate, said to the young man who bore his armor, "Come, let us go over to the Philistines' garrison that is on the other side." But he did not tell his father.

The two young warriors started off quite alone, made their way down from the heights before Gibeah, detoured around the encampment in the gorge, and began to climb the crags commanding the northern side of the pass on top of which was the Philistine garrison occupying the town.

The lookouts of the garrison saw them as they worked their way upward and challenged them, thinking them advance scouts of a guerrilla band of Benjaminites that had been hiding out in caves and holes to escape capture during the invasion.

As Jonathan and his armorbearer continued climbing, they were joined by some of the enslaved Benjaminites, and finally reaching the heights, Jonathan sprang among his enemies fighting like one possessed and cut them down to the number of twenty.

During the surprise and confusion, other captive laborers in the town above and in the camp below fell upon their enemies in outlying tents and in the separate straggling raiding parties.

When Saul's lookout reported that the people in the Philistine camp were apparently falling upon each other in savage fighting and the enemy on the fringes of the camp were trying to sneak away, Saul ordered a roll call to see who among his men were missing. When he discovered they were his own son and his armorbearer, Saul immediately commanded that the Ark of God be brought out and shown to the army. When the Israelites on the far side saw and heard the jubilation around the Ark, they interpreted it as a signal and all of the men of Benjamin even as far away as Mount Ephraim where many had been hiding, rose up and fell upon the invaders and cut them down.

"So the Lord saved Israel that day, and the battle passed over unto Beth-aven"—wherever exactly that was.

Saul followed up the retreating enemy until he had driven them back into their own territory and then, using the prestige of his victory, drew the people of Benjamin and Judah closer together under his authority by helping them thrust back from their borders the peoples of Ammon, Moab, and Edom, and even the distant Amalekites.

But the enmity between the Philistines and Israelites was too deep-seated and economic to be resolved permanently so long as both survived. The Philistines were not Semites although their god Dagon was a Semite deity which they had borrowed from the Canaanites—nor were they circumcised. Hemmed in by the sea on the west, Egypt on the south and the coastal holdings of Canaan on the north, the Philistines had nowhere to expand except into the mountains eastward and in that direction they ran headlong into the pastoral people of Judah who, in turn, had no elbow room except westward into Philistia.

The Philistines now put into effect a bold plan to cut in half the twelve tribes of the Yahweh amphictyony. They marched northward up the coast between the sand dunes and the hills and entered the Valley of Jezreel.

Saul could see a decision was imminent and yet because of his own jealousy the well-trained troops of David were not available to him. They were not available to the Philistines either, but lay inactive at remote Ziklag, for the Philistines did not dare risk calling on David to attack Saul.

As the Philistines swept eastward through the Valley of Jezreel, Saul awaited their attack on the slopes of Mount Gilboa. The event was disastrous for Saul whom Yahweh had forsaken. His sons were killed before his eyes, and, wounded, he died rather than fall into the hands of his enemies. Thus ended the tragic and short but turbulent and eventful reign of the first king of the Israelites.

David was saddened by the death of Saul, but crushed by the loss of Jonathan who had been like a brother to him. However, the event made David king of Judah in name if not in fact, for Samuel had already anointed him to be Saul's successor. Abner, Saul's captain, immediately sponsored Saul's son Ishbosheth, a Benjaminite, as Saul's successor and David was obliged once more to "look up to the hills whence cometh my help." In the hills above Hebron, where he had once hidden from Saul, still dwelt many of his loyal followers.

The situation had changed considerably since he had been an outlaw, for the Philistines now occupied much of the country claimed by Benjamin and the ten northern tribes, whose troops under Abner had been driven east of Jordan.

So David, beginning his struggle to maintain himself, found he was challenged on two fronts at once; physically, the Philistines were threatening him on the west and north, and politically, a son of Saul stood with an army against his alleged usurpation.

Intending to eliminate the house of Saul, David's nephew, Joab, murdered Abner who had come to negotiate a treaty, but David succeeded in convincing the people he had nothing to do with this treachery, or with the subsequent assassination of Ishbosheth. The remaining male of Saul's royal line was Jonathan's son who was a cripple and the northern tribes elected David to be their king.

At last the amphictyony of the twelve tribes of Israel, hitherto united in the worship of Yahweh, became also politically united under one ruler, a concentration of power which the Philistines looked upon with a jaundiced eye. After seven and a half years of ruling from Hebron, David felt confident enough to move northward to capture Jebus, the city of the Jebusites, which was more centrally located and more strongly situated than either Hebron or Bethlehem.

Finding the Ark rather neglected at Kirjath-jearim, David revitalized the Israelite amphictyony by bringing it to his new capital which he named Jerusalem, thus establishing the city as the central shrine of all Israel. This was a powerful step toward strengthening the political and military unification of the twelve tribes. As the Ark entered the city, David danced naked before it, to the annoyance of his wife.

One day in Jerusalem, early in his occupation of the city, David saw from his new palace roof a beautiful woman bathing herself on another rooftop. She was Bathsheba, the wife of Uriah the Hittite, and David wanted her desperately, so desperately that he sacrificed a force of soldiers in a hopeless attack on a walled city, after ordering Joab to put Uriah "in the forefront of the hottest battle." The death of Uriah made a widow of Bathsheba and relieved David—or so he thought—from the charge of adultery.

In spite of David's attempt to keep up appearances, Nathan, the prophet at the court of David, told him to his face that "the thing David had done displeased the Lord" and divine retribution was in store for him. He had not long to wait, for the first son his beloved Bathsheba bore him soon died.

The Philistines could not ignore the threat of David fortifying himself in Jerusalem for they too wanted to possess that almost impregnable mountain city. So, in self-preservation, the Philistines moved against the rising power of Israel. This time they struck close to their ultimate goal and occupied the Valley of Rephaim which cut into the mountains of Judah from the lowlands of the seacoast and made an excellent base of operations for cutting off any further movement by David to consolidate his southern military forces with those of the tribes to the north.

But David had served in the army of the Philistines and could now use against them his thorough knowledge of their method of waging war, just as centuries later the barbarians trained in Roman legions were to turn against their masters with success.

By gathering around him his augmented elite corps of warriors who had served him for years in all types of guerrilla operations, David had a mobile, flexible, well-co-ordinated, loyal, and disciplined force to use against the heavy, cumbersome forces of the Philistines, whose fighting men advanced behind iron shields that had to be carried by foot soldiers because they were too heavy to be carried by men wielding swords. It was a case of the lively boxer against the clumsy slugger.

So David, in his first engagement with his old enemy, not only defeated the Philistines but, in a series of vigorous attacks which he pressed home in their own territory, thrust them back behind the walls of their coastal cities. They never again became a serious threat to Israel, though for many generations there was an ebb and flow of struggle between the two peoples until finally the Philistines were absorbed by the races around them. They disappeared from history, leaving only their name to designate, ironically enough, a Semitic land—Palestine.

After chasing the Philistines to the sea, David built a chain of fortresses and strongholds to contain them on their shores, thus freeing himself to turn his attention to the organization of his kingdom and the security of its borders.

First David ended the independence of the principal cities commanding the strategic Valley of Jezreel—Megiddo, Taanach, and Beth-shan—by bringing them directly under his authority. He then divided his kingdom into districts and put administrators over them, accountable to him.

David was acquisitive and with his reign Israel and Yahweh came to glory. After subduing the Philistines he wanted to make the boundaries of his kingdom secure by incorporating his neighbors into his sphere of influence. Leading his strong military force of mercenaries, including even Philistines and Hittites, across the Jordan, he conquered Zobah, an important Aramaean state north of Damascus, taking a thousand chariots, seven thousand horsemen, and twenty thousand infantry. When the Syrians attempted to rescue Zobah, the Israelites killed twenty-two thousand of them and garrisoned Damascus.

Then the Edomites in the south grew restless and David moved against them promptly, killing eighteen thousand and garrisoning the country. As he marched against the Ammonites east of Jordan they called on the Syrians for help, but in vain, for David's army took seven thousand Syrian charioteers and forty thousand of their foot soldiers before occupying the Ammonite capital, Rabbath-Ammon (now Amman, chief city of Jordan). Inasmuch as there is no tactical account of how these battles were won, we may assume they were routine.

Incidentally, language was no serious barrier in administering such diverse peoples, for Syriac was a dialect of Aramaic, and the two were spoken from Mesopotamia to Edom. David allowed the Aramaic regions around Damascus to govern themselves, subject only to a viceroy of his choosing.

From all these conquests the tremendous booty of gold, silver, and brass was transported back to Jerusalem and stored in the treasury of the Temple. "And the fame of David went out into all lands; and the Lord brought the fear of him upon all nations" (Chron. 14:17).

And so under David, about 970 B.C., Israel reached the zenith of her military power and the greatest extent of territory in her long history. Yet for all his efforts, the two parts of his Israelite kingdom, though united physically, were spiritually never really merged. Even the common shrine at Jerusalem was referred to as "the Ark of Judah and Israel"—the tribes of the south and the north.

XI

THE REVOLT OF ABSALOM

AFTER DAVID had politically united the twelve tribes of the
Yahweh amphictyony and subjugated the nations on all frontiers,
it must have annoyed and dismayed him considerably when his
favorite son asked to share the administration of the kingdom he
had built.

Absalom was David's third son. His mother, Maacah, was the
daughter of the king of Geshur, which was a small territory of the

Aramaeans located in the west border of Bashan east northeast of the Sea of Galilee. Absalom was handsome and charming but ambitious and headstrong and, as events proved, he could carry a grudge a long time. For after his sister Tamar had been raped by their half-brother Amnon, Absalom bided his time for two years before he managed to arrange a suitable occasion for having Amnon assassinated. No sooner was this accomplished than he fled for safety to his maternal grandfather at Geshur where he stayed for three years before Joab (David's nephew and commander-in-chief) could effect a reconciliation with his royal father.

But David was determined not to divide or share his newly united kingdom with anyone, not even his favorite son, though he planned to make him his heir. David knew the impetuous young man was likely to take the law into his own hands. Moreover, Absalom belonged to a fanatical minority group called Nazirites who took a vow never to cut their hair or beards. Samson had also been a Nazirite.

Much as David loved his son, he could see that if Absalom were given authority prematurely he might draw apart from his father until, for all practical purposes, the kingdom would be divided again—perhaps in civil war. So David refused to divide his rule with Absalom.

Having failed to get what he wanted by open means, Absalom fell back on intrigue. When David was ill, or busy with government, or absent in war, Absalom stood in the gates of the capital and offered to sit in judgment on any case brought before him. In this way he made many friends throughout all Israel among those who came to the capital on business. Moreover, when he went on a journey, he went with horses and chariots and fifty men running before him, so that his prestige became great in the eyes of the people who now seldom saw their king. Absalom soon became the center of all those perennial malcontents and disappointed office-seekers who wanted a change in government for selfish reasons. In time a powerful underground conspiracy was formed with Absalom at its head and voluntary spies everywhere.

When the time for open rebellion drew near, Absalom asked David for permission to withdraw to Hebron in order to fulfill, so he said, a vow he had made at Geshur some years before. As soon as David gave his consent, Absalom went south on the pretext of holding sacrifices, taking with him one hundred warriors of the elite palace guard and many others. Spies went throughout Israel whispering that when the signal was given all should rise up and shout, "Absalom reigns in Hebron."

As soon as word of what was going on came to David, he realized he could not make a stand in Jerusalem without risking the destruction of the city and his new palace of cedar and stone, or even his own capture, so he fled eastward, across the Kidron, taking with him most of his household except a few concubines and accompanied by several hundred warriors many of whom had been with him since his guerrilla days in the time of Saul. Many of these were from Gath.

However, David left behind in Jerusalem several loyal adherents including the high priest Zadok and the counsellor Hushai. Hushai wanted to follow him, but David instructed him to mingle with the rebels in order to keep him informed of their plans and of everything that happened in Jerusalem after Absalom occupied the city. Ahimaaz, son of Zadok, was to be the messenger from Jerusalem to David.

Absalom behaved according to his nature and after entering Jerusalem pitched his tent on the roof of David's harem, thus announcing to all Israel the appropriation of his father's concubines, an irretrievable act for it signified the finality of Absalom's rebellion.

At this point a traitorous counsellor of David's advised Absalom that he could not be secure so long as his father remained alive, and Absalom consulted with Hushai as to whether and how he should bring about David's death.

This news Hushai passed on to Zadok who sent his son Ahimaaz with a full report to David.

Fearing now for his very life, David and the fugitives with him crossed the Jordan and turned northeastward to Mahanaim, a very strongly fortified city probably located somewhere near the Jabbok. This is the same Mahanaim where Saul's general Abner had proclaimed Saul's son, Ishbosheth, king instead of David. It was also the site of the legendary wrestling match between an angel and Jacob who was thereafter called Israel.

It is not without significance that David found this Ammonite stronghold, center of a former rebellion, now loyal to him in the present crisis. It is eloquent testimony to the wisdom, efficiency and general popularity of David's administration that the subjected peoples on his borders came to his support against the rebels among his own people and his own family.

The army of Absalom followed David across the Jordan, crossing further to the north, upstream, and moved into Gilead with Amasa as its general in place of Joab who had remained loyal to David. The two generals were cousins, so the impending battle would be quite a family affair.

The Ammonites and even the Gileadites now coming to David's support with troops and supplies, the royal anointed of Yahweh held a military review during which he divided his army into three parts with his nephew Joab commanding one, Abishai (Joab's brother) commanding another. To Ittai the Gittite— which is to say citizen of Gath—his old companion in arms, David gave the third part of his army which contained six hundred Philistine mercenaries. Altogether David's army numbered only about four thousand men, yet, although outnumbered, he decided to take the initiative.

But when David announced his intention of going forth into battle himself, the people raised strong objections, saying he was too old to defend himself personally and was too valuable to risk in the melee of combat. They insisted he remain with the reserves in Mahanaim whence he could go to the support of the army if the divisions were too hard pressed. David submitted to the popular will and stood by the gate of the city as his army went forth to battle. His parting command to his generals was to deal gently with Absalom.

Joab led the compact royal army forward and fell upon the rebel forces near the wood of Ephraim where the rebels fell into confusion among the trees and were cut down in great numbers by the disciplined troops of David.

Absalom was mounted on a mule, the animal considered suitable for royal or noble riders in those days, and as he dashed under an oak, he did not duck his head low enough to avoid the lowest branches. His long hair became wedged in the fork of a bough and his mule galloped out from under him leaving the Nazirite dangling there helplessly, an obvious symbol of Yahweh's intervention and His disapproval of a son who raised his hand against his father and the Lord's anointed.

A soldier of Joab's division, seeing the king's son hanging by his hair, ran to his commander with the news. When Joab asked why he had not killed him, the man said he could not raise his hand against the king's son. But Joab had no such compunction. Taking up three darts he drove them into his cousin's body. Then the ten officers of Joab's staff who bore his armor killed the still breathing rebel.

Cutting Absalom down, they threw him into a deep pit and piled stones upon him, spreading through the rebel host word of what had happened. On hearing that their leader was dead and their cause lost, the rebels fled in panic.

At the end of the day, when Joab called off the bloody pursuit

Ahimaaz asked to be the first to tell the news of the victory to King David. Joab refused him because he had always been the bearer of good news and any report of the battle would have to include the death of Absalom. So he sent Cushi instead.

The eager Ahimaaz was not to be thwarted. By taking a short-cut, he reached David first. Only after he had told of the victory did he realize the superior wisdom and kindness of Joab, for David asked at once about Absalom. Ahimaaz equivocated. He said there had been a commotion, but he had not seen exactly what it had been about.

Cushi at this moment running up, David asked, "Is the young man Absalom safe?"

And Cushi answered, "The enemies of my lord the king and all that rise against thee to do thee hurt, be as that young man is."

David wept and went alone up into a tower to mourn deeply and bitterly.

It is evident from this account that the Bible is always more concerned with human relationships and human behavior than with tactics. The cause and the result are the major concerns of the chroniclers.

At last Joab persuaded David to end his lamenting and come down from his tower to shoulder again the heavy burden of government. The rebellion was over, the conspiracy broken up, the kingdom preserved intact and in peace, and the way paved for the resplendent reign of Solomon.

On his deathbed, perhaps with some misgivings, David called to him his heir, Bathsheba's son, saying:

"Be strong and show yourself a man. Keep the charge of the Lord your God, walking in his ways, keeping his statutes, and his commandments, and his judgments, and his testimonies, as it is written in the law of Moses, that you may prosper in all you do and wherever you go."

XII

THE FATE OF SAMARIA

Solomon kept a large standing army though he fought no wars and made no conquests. His reign was a period of peace—and decay. Under an outward show of wealth, splendor and prosperity, slowly and little by little the strong and closely knit administration left by David loosened and began to fall apart at the seams.

In spite of his reputation for wisdom, Solomon was not wise when he showed partiality for Judah in allocating taxes to pay for the cost of his palatial building program and the lavish displays that so impressed the Queen of Sheba. When Solomon discriminated against the ten northern tribes of the amphictyony, grinding them down under heavy taxes while the people of Judah enjoyed many exemptions, he drove the entering wedge between the two regions.

Moreover, shrewd and able as Solomon might have been in politics and international diplomacy, he did not inherit the feeling of intimacy with Yahweh that was one of the dominant characteristics of his father David. As a result, the priesthood, in spite of the splendors of the Temple Solomon had built for them to worship in, drew back in fear that so much palace apostasy and so many foreign, imported harem gods (Solomon had married a daughter of Pharaoh) might bring reprisals from the jealous Yahweh.

The first crevice to appear in the great bulwark David had built around the kingdom appeared for all to see, but went unrepaired. The Aramaean leader Rezon drove out of Damascus the governor David had appointed to represent him there. David would have taken steps at once, but Solomon found the incident too insignificant to bother him. It was the first bite out of his empire; unchallenged and uncorrected it could very well lead to ultimate disaster.

After Solomon's death Judah recognized his son Rehoboam as king, for the house of David was Judaean, but for the oppressed ten northern tribes it was another matter. They elected their kings, as they had elected David. They had accepted Solomon, but they wanted tax relief and especially relief from forced labor in lieu of taxes, so they rejected Rehoboam and elected Jeroboam who had been an administrator under Solomon and was designated by the prophet Ahijah of sacred Shiloh to rule over Israel.

The northern tribes now decided to be less dependent on the shrine of Yahweh at Jerusalem. They set up two shrines so that their people would not have to travel all the way to Jerusalem and the wealth of the north that would have gone to Jerusalem was siphoned off into the new shrines. One of these was at the city of Dan which had long been a sacred place far to the north and had its own priesthood; the other was founded at Bethel on the road to Jerusalem and only a dozen miles north of it. This one had to be supplied with a new priesthood since the Levites who once lived there had withdrawn to serve in the Temple at Jerusalem.

So the rift that began as political quickly became religious as well and the country was divided between the ten tribes of Israel in the north and Judah, which had absorbed the tribes of Benjamin and Dan, in the south. The division widened rapidly. Judah remained loyal to the ritual of the Temple but the north became heretical, introducing new foreign forms of worship and politically descending to bloody expedients of assassination and usurpation.

There ensued for two centuries almost incessant boundary disputes and civil war between the north and the south; a string of forts in the land of Benjamin was built to defend Jerusalem. The north even tried to get the Egyptian Pharaoh Shishonk (Shishak) to help them, but Judah bought the Egyptian off with the Temple treasure.

The full chronicles of these events have been lost and only meager data is available, but it seems that at one period Egypt pushed up the coast, bypassing Judah, and drove Israel out of much of its territory. For a time, Israel established a capital in lands east of the Jordan.

But eventually a great leader became king of the northern tribes and Israel had a renaissance under Omri. He built a magnificent and "very strong hold" on Mount Shemer and called it Samaria and, to cement his ties with the sea towns of Phoenicia, he married his son Ahab to the princess Jezebel, daughter of the king of Tyre. To the sumptuous new capital at Samaria, Jezebel brought her cult of Baal and the introduction of the pagan bull, symbol of fertility, began to confuse and debauch the pure cult of Yahweh who was thought of in Israel as being invisibly enthroned on golden calves, although in the Temple at Jerusalem he was enthroned on two seraphim.

This was the period of Elijah and Elisha and their religious conflicts with the priests of Baal, which ended in the massacre of four hundred and fifty of them.

There were brief intervals when Israel and Judah lived in peace with one another but most of the time was spent in skirmishing and battling, to the consequent weakening of both sides.

They could hardly have chosen a worse era in which to tear one another to pieces. They would soon have need of all the wealth and unity David and Solomon had provided for them, for after several generations of weakness the ambitious power of Assyria regained enough strength to take the offensive again and extend once more the boundaries of its empire, even aiming to include Egypt.

Palestine, of course, lay in its way.

As prologue to a new series of invasions, Hazael, king of Syria and Damascus, raided down the coast as far as Gath which he looted. Then he looked eastward toward Jerusalem but King Joash of Judah saved himself and his capital by himself looting the Temple treasure to buy off the Syrian. This treasure had been accumulated by the faithful from all Palestine and even beyond its borders, and the use of it for the benefit of Judah was a contributory cause of the continuing political defection of the northern tribes and increased emphasis on their own local shrines.

The bickering and fighting flared up again and again but the history is confusing to follow. Both north and south had kings named Joram and also Joash and the Biblical accounts are difficult to follow and keep chronologically in order. It is simpler to turn to the more orderly records of Assyria and Egypt—so long as we make allowances for the writers' lively aptitude for braggadocio, bombast, and exaggeration. From them we have a fairly definite chronological account of the two nations' dealings with Israel and Judah, and cross reference can be made with passages in II Kings.

Now began a chain of events the outcome of which Isaiah saw clearly (Is. 8:1–4).

About 860 B.C. Shalmaneser III, king of Assyria, a leader with boundless ambition, energy, and ability, rose like a star in the east and began pushing forward along the northern curve of the Euphrates into the territory of the Hittites who had been a world power since 1450 B.C. He overran the Hittites as far as the Mediterranean and swept them into oblivion. After taking the rich copper mines of Cilicia he turned, poised for a swoop down into Syria.

Forewarned of his approach, the kings of Syria and Israel patched up a quick peace and united against their common enemy. The two forces met head on at Qarqar on the Orontes River in 854 B.C. The Syrian king had an army of twenty thousand men, twelve hundred horses, and twelve hundred chariots. King Ahab of Israel had a force of ten thousand men and two thousand chariots. These were only two contingents of troops by twelve kings federated against Assyria, so even by today's standards the total number of men engaged is impressive. The logistical problem of feeding and supplying such a large force by means of asses and ox carts is frightening to contemplate.

No mention of this bloody battle appears in the Bible, for the interests of the Lord God Yahweh were not considered to be involved. So literate a nation as ancient Israel undoubtedly at one time had a complete account of its historical events and such a record is more than once referred to by the compilers and editors of the religious books, Judges, Kings, and Chronicles, who were selecting material from it with a single religious purpose in mind. Unfortunately this source material has not yet come to light. Whether it was lost during the later destructions of Jerusalem, or hidden where it has not yet been found, no one knows.

But according to the Assyrian account the Orontes was dammed with the dead of Syria and Israel. Even so, it was not the end, for Shalmaneser had to return again and again to attack before he succeeded in putting King Jehu, Ahab's successor, under tribute.

Alarmed into a show of good sense, Jehu of Israel and Hazael of Syria united to meet the menace of Shalmaneser. Then, fortunately for the makeshift and shaky federation, a rebellion in Assyria against Shalmaneser gave them a breathing spell.

It seems an incomprehensible idiocy, but with such a menace

still looming in the east, Syria used this respite to fall upon Israel and seize some territory. Assyria recovered partially from internal disorder to take time and energy to harass Syria. Whereupon Israel took advantage of the opportunity to retake the lands so recently lost.

About the year 800 B.C. increasing pressures on the borders of Judah inspired King Uzziah greatly to strengthen the walls and fortifications of Jerusalem. A considerable irrigation system was constructed to increase the productivity of the land and add to the defenses by supplying the people of the city with more water.

Meanwhile Judah pushed its frontier southward toward Egypt. In fact, Judah became strong enough to regain the region of the Arabah as far as the Gulf of Aqaba where it fortified Elah and the gulf ports needed for shipping copper from the smelters there. To effect all this the army had been reorganized and a ring of forts built around Jerusalem.

As though for an omen, at this time there occurred a very violent earthquake that shifted great masses of land and dramatically cracked the walls of the Temple from the roof to the foundations.

Now, too, for a brief moment among the eons of time, Israel in the north had a final period of glory under King Jeroboam II (c. 783–742 B.C., though authorities differ), while Egypt, having subsided in exhaustion after the aggressive campaigns of Shishonk, lapsed into inactivity and thus relieved Palestine from pressure on the southern border.

But the hopeful outlook did not last long. Another phenomenon rose in the east, this time no star but a veritable sun, for in 745 B.C. Tiglath-pileser (the same man called Pul in II Kings 15:19) seized the throne of Assyria and for the next eighteen years that ruthless people had the greatest king they had ever known.

During a period of adjustment while he consolidated his power,

99

Tiglath-pileser was content to accept tribute from the Temple treasure but only as a temporary expedient. He had an ambition to dominate the world and in his mind there was a simple method of achieving it. After conquering a people he deported them en masse and brought in to fill the vacuum an equal number of people from some other part of his vast empire, which soon included most of what is now known as Asia Minor. In this way he intended to break up national and racial units and blend them all together into one great homogeneous population that would know only one country, one emblem, one god, and one king.

In the year 736 he was ready to begin his campaign to rule the world.

In the teeth of a cataclysm, the leaders of Israel had been recklessly engaging in a turmoil of assassinations and usurpations while the Assyrian winged beast stalked toward them and the prophets of Israel cried themselves hoarse in warning, but in vain. Israel and Syria made valiant efforts to bribe the approaching aggressor to keep away, to spare their lands. It was like trying to bribe with coins a hungry python to abstain from devouring its helpless, fleshy prey.

The great prophet Isaiah, thoroughly impressed by the Assyrian successes, began to warn his people to stop their outrageous civil bickering and vainglorious wars, to unite before God punished them for their disunity and their betrayal of the covenant of the twelve tribes of the amphictyony which guarded His shrine and preserved His worship. But the children of Israel and Judah were smugly lulled into a false sense of security by paying an indemnity to the Assyrians; they turned a deaf ear to Isaiah, heedless that their God might turn a deaf ear to them also.

Three years quickly passed and then Pekah, who had become king of Israel by the shortcut of assassination, formed a new coalition with Rezin, who was king of Damascus, to make a common front against the encroaching power of Assyria. This time they invited Ahaz of Judah to join them. He refused. Angered, they marched on Jerusalem to force his compliance. Ahaz rashly invited the wild winged bull of Assyria into his house by calling on Tiglath-pileser for help, and paying for it out of the Temple treasure. It was a dangerously shortsighted policy but the prophets of the Lord cried out against it unheeded.

Tiglath-pileser crushed Damascus and then, crossing the upper Jordan north of the Sea of Galilee, captured Kadesh and Hazor, deporting the inhabitants to the banks of the far-distant Tigris and bringing in people from other parts of his empire to take their places. Then tearing through the northern lands, devastating and deporting, he spared only the region of Mt. Ephraim and Samaria.

But not for long. The way had been prepared for the first great disaster to fall upon the twelve tribes of the Yahweh amphictyony. Consolidating his gains, Tiglath-pileser laid siege to Samaria itself, proudly walled on its high hill, rising entirely isolated in the middle of a bowl of fertile hills and valleys and commanding the intersection of strategic highways.

The stronghold of Samaria (later renamed Sebaste by Herod) from its vigorous beginning under Omri had by this time become very strong indeed. It boasted a population of thirty thousand souls. Recent excavations have uncovered walls of massive proportions, running in some places to a thickness of thirty-three feet, constructed with heavy blocks of masonry and casemated with vaulted chambers, all of which explains in part why the city held out so long. The inhabitants too were apparently as stubborn, tough, and inflexible as their rugged walls. Tiglath-pileser died in the progress of the siege and the slow, painful process of reducing such a fortification was taken up by his successor, Sargon II.

The siege of Samaria lasted for three years, yet that is about all we know concerning it. In II Kings, 17:5–6 we are told:

"Then the king of Assyria came up throughout all the land, and went up to Samaria, and besieged it three years. In the ninth year of Hoshea the king of Assyria took Samaria, and carried Israel away into Assyria, and placed them in Halah, and in Habor by the river of Gozan, and in the cities of the Medes."

We can only surmise that the details of the siege must have been eventful and dramatic beyond any other siege of any other city in its time and yet no detailed account can be found. If it was recorded by the Assyrian chroniclers that record has not yet come to light. Perhaps the taking of Samaria reflected little credit on the victors and so they were silent about it. Indeed, there is reason to believe from allusions dropped here and there by the prophets that no one wanted to remember it, for the people held out so long in the face of starvation that they were forced to resort to cannibalism; it was hinted that even little children were eaten. In any case, the people of Samaria were considered by Judaeans to be schismatics and heretics and outside the pale of the true worship of Yahweh as preserved at Jerusalem. Because they were a people from whom God had turned his face, they were dropped from the southern sources of the Bible. The northern sources, of course, came to an end with the deportation and obliteration of the northern tribes.

It is also likely that the Assyrian besiegers were too numerous for their own good and camping so long in one location under conditions that could hardly have been sanitary by any standards, they fell victim to decimating plagues. Great numbers can be an encumbrance to an army living off the land so far from home, and the besiegers might have needed food and been forced to relax the siege from time to time in order to survive.

Whatever the details may have been, after a ghastly three years Samaria fell and its great fortifications were pulled down. The chief citizens—the leaders, landowners, and artisans—to the number of twenty-seven thousand two hundred and ninety, according to Assyrian record, were deported and scattered over the far-flung face of the Assyrian earth, even as far as the cities of the Medes near the Caspian Sea. And into their vacated homes came immigrants transplanted from Babylon (Iraq), Elam (Iran), and Syria. The ten northern tribes of Israel were never heard of again.

Only the two tribes of Judah and Benjamin remained of the once ambitious and extensive, but now shrunken Israelite amphictyony that guarded the shrine and worship of Yahweh in Jerusalem.

XIII

THE SIEGE OF JERUSALEM

JERUSALEM, the capital of Judah, one of the highest cities in ancient history, was on a rocky hill about twenty-six hundred feet above sea level. Its height was all the more dramatic because the Mediterranean Sea was only thirty-three miles due west, while, a mere fourteen miles to the east, the Dead Sea lay simmering thirty-eight hundred feet below the rugged, precipitous Judaean wilderness.

Jerusalem was altogether unique for such an important city. It was remote. It had no river, no harbor, and though centrally located it was on no trade route, at no commercial crossroads. It was a fortress protecting a shrine and its treasure. On the other hand, for pilgrims or invaders, it was accessible by means of a few small defensible valleys that led up to the ridge from the coastal plain on the west.

The oldest part of Jerusalem was the small rock plateau used by Araunah for a threshing floor, bought from him by David and on which Solomon built his Temple to Yahweh. This table rock, the original Zion, was on the northern part of the oval hill Ophel (also later included in the name Zion) where David founded his walled city. Although the site was half a mile above sea level, it was not the highest part of the mountain ridge. There was higher ground to the west and during the reigns of the kings of Judah the city spread westward over these slopes to the summit where generations later Herod built his towers, his palace, and gardens. In later times, the word Zion also included this area.

The Temple enclosure itself was well fortified for defensive strength. On the east the massive walls of stone dropped steeply down into the Kidron Valley which was many feet deeper in the time of Hezekiah, before centuries of rubble had been tumbled into it after repeated destructions. On the west of the Temple was a depression that ran south to join the Kidron where it met the Hinnom Valley that ran along the far western side of the main ridge. A supply of water was always a crucial problem in those days for there were only two sources. One was the average twenty-six inch rainfall between November and April, which was caught by drains and channels leading it to huge underground cisterns where it was stored to be tapped during the parching summer droughts. The other source was a modest flow from the spring Gihon located in a cave on the east slope of Ophel outside the wall of the City of David. This water was collected in a pool built by Solomon from which conduits irrigated the king's kitchen garden, but this pool was outside the walls of the city. Although in Solomon's reign Judah reached its highest period of peace and prosperity, the reservoirs, called Solomon's pools, some miles beyond the city, probably were built sometimes between Solomon's reign and the second century before Christ.

As the city grew in size and population under the kings of Judah, the walls were greatly extended and strengthened. They were an impressive sight. The rose-buff stone, the many towers and fortified gates glowed with mystic beauty in the level sunlight and were climaxed in splendor by the lofty Temple overlaid with gold.

The climate was pleasant with an average mean temperature of sixty-three degrees. Of course it was hot in the summer midday sun but in the evening cool winds blew in from the Mediterranean not far away and the people found comfortable relief by living under awnings spread atop their flat mud roofs. Some years the winters were severe, with snow and biting wind. For good reasons had Araunah used the rock on the edge of the cliff above the Kidron for a threshing floor—the chaff blew fast and far, eastward toward the Mount of Olives.

Although the capital was on no caravan route and lacked any natural source of wealth, Jerusalem was not without thriving and lucrative commerce. The Temple itself was Jerusalem's chief industry. Israelites came from all over the eastern world, from Palestine, Asia, and Egypt to pay tribute and buy in the Temple grounds the flawless animals and doves which alone were acceptable by priestly law for sacrifice to Yahweh. A constant flow of the faithful making pilgrimage passed through the city, which during the great festivals was crammed almost beyond endurance with families squatting in the streets and bivouacking by thousands outside the walls. Consequently the treasure of the Temple, though depleted many times, was always fabulous. To aggressive hostile invaders, the wealth locked up in Jerusalem was inevitably a constant and irresistible temptation.

Sennacherib, the son of Sargon II, came to the throne of Assyria in 705 B.C., and was, according to J. H. Breasted, "One of the great statesmen of the early Orient." (C. W. Ceram calls him "half-mad.") While he was busy bringing back to obedience the defecting neighboring peoples of Babylon and Chaldaea, the tributary nations of the west rebelled and, shaking off their financial shackles, turned to Egypt for support. It was the old familiar pattern repeated. One of these restless rebels against Assyria was Hezekiah, the king of Judah, caught up in a power squeeze, as though in a vise, between the compressing elements of Assyria and Egypt.

After conquering all the kings east of Jordan and the Dead Sea in one campaign, Sennacherib in the next moved westward from Nineveh and descended on Damascus. Reaching the Mediterranean, he isolated the island fortress of Tyre. He then continued south, taking Joppa and the Phoenician cities down the coast as far as Ashdod and Ashkelon whose king, with all his family, was deported to Assyria. This brought the Assyrian power to the borders of Egypt, the only power strong enough to challenge effectively Sennacherib's imperial dream of world domination, but the son of Sargon dared not advance farther while the fortified centers of Judah were left intact behind him. Therefore, as soon as he had taken the strongly walled city of Lachish that stood in his way, he faced toward Jerusalem which lay solitary and friendless before and above him. Hezekiah had called on the ruler of Egypt and Ethiopia for help in vain.

An Assyrian chronicler writing after 689 B.C. recorded in stone the bombastic boasts and jubilant arrogance of the Assyrian king.

"As for Hezekiah of Judah, he did not submit to my yoke: forty-six of his strong cities, fortresses and countless small towns in the vicinity, I besieged and conquered by building earthworks, by bringing up siege-engines, with the help of assault troops, by breaches in the walls, by mines under the ramparts and onslaughts with the battering-ram. I deported from among them and counted as spoil two hundred thousand one hundred and fifty persons, young and old, men and women, and horses, mules, asses, camels, sheep and cattle in countless numbers." Thus in part boasts Sennacherib, as translated by J. T. Nelis, from one of the hexagonal clay prisms that have been uncovered by archaeologists.

But these events also occurred in the days of the first Isaiah, that wise, learned, and far-seeing seer. Usually, it seems, God saw fit to speak to man through the mouths of those who could understand His meaning and His laws and make them clear to ordinary mortals. It was obvious to a man of intelligence and vision, like Isaiah, that large armies were frequently their own worst enemy. Armies can be defeated by overwhelming numbers alone—even by their own excessive numbers. Large armies starve, it is said. Then, too, when large armies concentrate in a small area, sanitary precautions break down and disease can kill more men than bows and arrows, swords and spears, or even treachery. And so Isaiah raised his voice and spoke.

"Thus says the Lord, the Lord of Hosts: O my people who dwell in Zion be not afraid of the Assyrians when they smite with the rod and lift up their staff against you as the Egyptians did. For in a very little while my indignation will come to an end, and my anger will be directed to their destruction and in that day his burden will depart from your shoulder and his yoke will be destroyed from your neck" (Is. 10:24–27).

Hezekiah, knowing full well the eagerness of the Assyrian king to move on into Egypt before the winter rains and spring floods, took advantage—or so he thought—of Sennacherib's impatience and offered a rich ransom to redeem Jerusalem from imminent pillage and destruction. It was an example of a kind of international blackmail not unknown in the world today.

Again a king of Judah raided the Temple treasure in order to save Jerusalem.

Sennacherib accepted the ransom, which would buy mercenaries, for he needed as large a force as he could muster to attack Egypt in her sacred home precincts. But, master of the double cross, when he marched southward he left behind him Rabshakeh, a general, with a force large enough to besiege the city that had in its folly tried to trade with a ruthless and unprincipled enemy.

Hezekiah, however, had not been foolish enough to rely entirely on happy optimism in the face of Sennacherib's menacing approach, and while the Assyrians were busy with the capture of the cities of Judah and Benjamin, Jerusalem was made more secure. The walls, already strong, were made stronger. But more especially the water supply was brought to the city from the spring Gihon through a tunnel leading circuitously under the walls and emptying into a pool within their protecting enclosure.

The underground canal was an ingenious piece of engineering. To save time, which was of the essence, diggers began cutting through the solid rock from both ends of the projected tunnel simultaneously. A gravity flow had to be maintained but the cut could not be made in a straight line. For the sake of speed, every advantage had to be taken of any soft fissure encountered in the rock. Moreover, the water tunnel led under the old City of David where many noble Israelites had been buried and care had to be taken not to cut through their tombs.

Considering the fact that the zigzagging tunnel is seventeen thousand and forty-nine feet long (about two feet wide and five feet high), it is remarkable that the two working parties arrived at a point exactly opposite one another. This was in the year 701 B.C. Recently a memorial inscription was discovered carved in a cursive Hebrew lettering which is in itself a work of art:

"The boring through is completed. Now this is the story of the boring through. While the workmen were still lifting pick to pick, each toward his neighbor, and while three cubits remained to be cut through, each heard the voice of the other who called his neighbor, since there was a crevice in the rock on the right side. And on the day of the boring through the stonecutters struck, each to meet his fellow, pick to pick; and there flowed the waters to the pool for a thousand and two hundred cubits, and a hundred cubits was the height of the rock above the heads of the stone-cutters."

Thus was the main water supply brought into the city where the women of Jerusalem could reach it in comparative safety by going down thirty-three steps cut into the solid rock. It was a wise precaution, for when the Assyrians invested the city they sewed it up tight. No human being could enter into it or escape out of the walls.

Hezekiah was in dire straits, as witness the boastful account of Sennacherib: "Himself I shut up in Jerusalem his royal city like a bird in its cage. Earthworks I threw up against him: the one coming out of the city gate I turned back to his misery."

Apparently the Assyrian forces under Rabshakeh had been impatiently bivouacked around the city, waiting for famine to do its work for them within the walls. But they were sorely needed in Egypt which, though powerless to send a force to relieve Jerusalem, was giving Sennacherib a bad time. And even besiegers can get hungry.

Rabshakeh sent word to Hezekiah to come out from behind his walls and parley. The king of Judah feared betrayal and refused. Instead he sent an ambassador, one Eliakim. Apparently the ambassador himself did not venture too close to the Assyrians, but kept at a discreet shouting distance, for when Rabshakeh warned him that Hezekiah could not possibly defend the city indefinitely against the might of Assyria and that the people would be wise to force him to submit, he spoke in Hebrew so the defenders could hear and understand him.

But Eliakim replied in Syriac so the Hebrew defenders could not follow his argument.

Then Rabshakeh taunted the Judaeans, shouting, "I will give you two thousand horses if you can find so many horsemen to put on their backs."

This was apparently not worth answering for no further record was made of it. The Hebrews had no notion of dashing out in a suicidal sortie and certainly had no desire to stable such a herd in the starving city. Because of their religion they could not even use the beasts for food.

Perhaps another known factor stiffened the stubborn defense of the city. The Assyrians were notorious for their cruelty, which seems remarkable in a time when cruelty was commonplace. And yet even fear of Assyrian brutality was not the chief reason the people of Judah held Jerusalem so tenaciously; they were custodians of the Temple of Yahweh and no son of Israel wanted to survive if survival meant that the House and abode of their God were defiled.

After the open-air diplomatic exchange, Hezekiah became dismayed and asked Isaiah for prayers and sacrifices for the salvation of the city and people, which indicates that Isaiah himself was within the walls.

Moreover, about this time, Sennacherib had written to Hezekiah to open his gates at once or on his triumphant return out of Egypt he would utterly destroy him. It seems probable that Sennacherib was in urgent need of reinforcement by the troops tied down before Jerusalem.

Although Isaiah had warned Hezekiah against putting his trust in the sly, waning power of Egypt, while rebelling against the ferocious power of Assyria merely because Sennacherib had been preoccupied for a time with political upheavals at home, the prophet now spoke words of comfort. Seeing the host crowded into camps around the city, and knowing that the frustrated Sennacherib, unable to subjugate Egypt, would be forced by the season and the elements to retreat into Judah and add his great army to the forces of the besiegers, Isaiah said:

"He shall not come to this city or shoot an arrow there, or come before it with shield or cast up a mound against it. By the way he came, by the same he shall return."

It was clear to such a wise man what would happen when the army of Sennacherib joined the encampment of Rabshakeh. But, although the chronicles of the Assyrian historians are vague about this, apparently the disaster of congestion fell upon the Assyrians even before Sennacherib reached the Judaean highlands. Be that as it may, suddenly, during the night, plague struck the Assyrian camp before Jerusalem with almost unprecedented viciousness. Invisible germs did what the armament of empire had been unable to effect. The Assyrians died in the night by thousands and then by tens of thousands. The Biblical account definitely puts the loss at one hundred eighty-five thousand. Without wasting a moment, the Assyrians struck camp and hurriedly departed, making their way as best they could back to Nineveh, leaving their mounds of dead behind them. So it befell exactly as Isaiah had prophesied.

Further disasters awaited the Assyrians, but perils also lurked unsuspected in the tempestuous future of Judah.

XIV

THE FALL OF JERUSALEM

A BRIEF TIME of respite for Judah followed a defeat inflicted on the Assyrian army by the Medes who held lands adjoining Assyria on the northeast. By this victory the Medes established their independence. Whereupon the Semitic Chaldaeans on the south near the mouth of the Euphrates also rose up against Assyria and gained a measure of independence. These disturbances kept the Assyrian army busy in the east.

The Chaldaeans were a people far advanced in civilization, as recent excavations around Ur have eloquently demonstrated. They were brilliant astronomers who kept unbroken records of the heavenly bodies for nearly four centuries and computed the year within less than half an hour of its now known length. This was the place and these were the people whence the ancestors of Israel come.

As soon as a measure of stability had been established in the Euphrates-Tigris region (Mesopotamia), the Chaldaean king of Babylon, Merodach-baladan, sent an embassy to Jerusalem to see how the king of Judah was adjusting himself to the new political situation in the East and whether the fickle and inept Hezekiah might be persuaded to form an alliance with the Chaldaeans against Assyria.

Hezekiah had learned nothing from experience or from Isaiah. He foolishly took the ambassadors on a tour of the Temple and boastfully showed them the Temple arsenal and treasury. In spite of the raids that had been made on it, the Temple treasure was still fabulous. It made the ambassadorial eyes goggle for it was a sight not to be forgotten.

The stupidity of Hezekiah on this occasion so infuriated Isaiah that he uttered a warning blast against the reckless head of the Yahweh amphictyony. In an outburst of anger and despair, he said: "Behold, the days come, that all that is in thine house, and that which thy fathers have laid up in store unto this day, shall be carried into Babylon: nothing shall be left, saith the Lord."

In Isaiah's view it was Yahweh who had sent against Judah the Assyrian sharp-shooting archers and fast light cavalry and solid masses of disciplined infantry as a rod to chastise His erring children.

The prophets never lost sight of the basic strength of Judah as keepers of the Temple at Jerusalem, knowing that without unity of faith and purpose their small numbers would be impotent against their stronger neighbors. Of the great days of the Yahweh amphictyony only the tribes of the descendants of Judah and

Benjamin remained. All the other children of Jacob—who had been renamed Israel after his spiritual rebirth—were gone, even the descendants of Joseph were utterly vanished, swallowed up in the melting pot of intermarriage with other Semitic and non-Semitic peoples.

But from time to time stupid kings and self-seeking leaders forgot what it was that held the Yahweh amphictyony together and went traipsing off after the false gods of the benighted peoples who surrounded them, whose women they married and brought into their homes, idols and all. The story of King Ahab and his wife Jezebel of Tyre was the classic example and prototype of what happened over and over again.

This was not the only method of straying from the Covenant and falling from grace, however. When Hezekiah's son Manasseh came to the throne of Judah in 687, he set about slaughtering priests and prophets in numbers that made Molech's (Moloch or Molok) human sacrifices seem almost abstemious. Though the young king's mother, Hepzibah, was a native of Jerusalem, her royal son was only twelve years old, so she must take the blame for his relapse into the worship of Baal and Astarte, and the murder of the priests of Yahweh. His apostasy reached a peak when he revived the sadistic brutality of delivering infants into the red-hot brass hands and fiery maw of Molech. It considerably dismayed the chroniclers of Judah that the reign of this wicked and depraved king was marked by half a century of peace and prosperity. Only the Book of Job can account for it.

The prophets, especially Isaiah and Micah, were loud and frequent in their warnings that treason to Yahweh would not go unpunished indefinitely, that it would even finally bring about the destruction of Jerusalem. So desperate was the ancient historians' plight that they slipped into Chronicles (II Chron. 33) an apparently apochryphal effort to account for the happy prosperity of the reign of so godless a king as Manasseh by relating his ultimate repentance. But the later Rabbinical literature asserts Manasseh had Isaiah sawed in half and thereby inevitably laid Judah open to punishment.

It was during Manasseh's reign that Assyria annexed Egypt and after Esar-haddon died in 668 or 669 B.C. his son and successor Ashurbanipal occupied the Nile valley as far up as Thebes (modern Luxor) and finally, to discipline the rebellious Egyptians, destroyed Thebes in 661 B.C. This same year, incidentally, was the year in which the great magi of Iran, Zoroaster (Greek for Zarathustra) was born. But the ascendancy of Assyria over Egypt was short-lived, coming to an end only five years after the destruction of Thebes.

Amon, the son of Manasseh, was a chip off the old execution block and his reign was shortened to a few months when he was assassinated by his own palace staff. The people of Jerusalem, however, were still loyal to the House of David; by killing the killers they put Amon's eight-year-old son Josiah on the throne about the year 640 B.C.

The boy was quite different from his father and grandfather, reflecting instead the best qualities of his ancestor David in both religious and administrative behavior. It was during Josiah's noble reign that the so-called Books of Moses were discovered in the Temple treasury, whereupon the king convoked all the priests and Levites and read to them the holy admonitions. From this event sprang a great religious revival. Josiah quickly purged the cult of Yahweh of all heresies, returned Judah to the exclusive worship of Yahweh and repaired His neglected Temple. Pagan shrines and groves were torn down and all priests who had been idolatrous were executed, saving only those members of the family of Aaron who had strayed and recanted. Josiah published a code of economic reforms and reorganized the army. His reign was Judah's Indian summer, its calm before the tempest. Soon the chilling hand of Babylon would cast a long shadow over the land.

This happy time in Judah drew to a close not long after the rise of the Aramaean prince Nabopolassar of the Semitic Chaldaeans who lived in Lower Mesopotamia. Nabopolassar formed an alliance with the Medes whose kingdom was northeast of the Assyrian domain in Upper Mesopotamia. Together these two forces overthrew the Assyrian power and in 612 B.C. completely and for all time destroyed Nineveh whose dazzling architectural glories and high civilization vanished almost overnight into rubble. Fortunately for us, in this rubble and practically intact was the great clay library of ancient lore collected by the scholarly King Ashurbanipal, which has been uncovered and translated in our own time.

The Pharaoh Necho of Egypt now thought he saw his opportunity to restore the former boundaries of his empire and seize supreme world power. The defeated king of Assyria was still trying to hold out at Haran on the upper Euphrates and Necho decided to march to his help and thus check the rising power that was centering its administration in Babylon.

On his way up the Mediterranean coast the Egyptian first took Gaza and then Ashkelon, in his hurry bypassing Judah. But when Necho came to the Valley of Jezreel, he found Josiah with an army drawn up across his path with the intention of stopping him at Megiddo.

Necho had no time to waste. Accounts differ as to whether he called Josiah into conference or into battle but the result was the same: Josiah was shot with an arrow and died of the wound.

The Babylonian army defeated both the Assyrians and the Egyptians but, as it was unable to follow up its victory, Necho took over the kingdom of Syria. Deciding to take care of the

Judaean situation now festering between his new dominion and Egypt, and fearing to trust Josiah's son Jehoahaz, Necho deposed him, took him as hostage to Egypt, where he later died, and made his brother Eliakim king instead. To demonstrate to all that the new king of Judah was only a puppet of Egypt, the Pharaoh changed his name to Jehoiakim.

The triumphant Semitic dynasty rising in the east developed its capital of Babylon until it rivaled and even surpassed the former Nineveh in glory. Babylonian plans for expansion were not handicapped by any need to consider the ambitions of the Medes who preferred to stay in their own lands and so when the Babylonians found a new leader in the commanding personality of Nebuchadnezzar the Great, son of Nabopolassar, he was able to act with complete independence.

The new king of Babylon, who was to rule forty-three years, headed at once for Syria, met Necho at Carchemish on the upper Euphrates in 605 B.C. and decisively defeated him. With this victory all the country of Syria fell under Nebuchadnezzar's control as far as the borders of Judah which he promptly put under tribute.

After consolidating his gains under his own administration, Nebuchadnezzar continued southward along the coast and invaded Egypt.

Mistaking this for an opportunity, King Jehoiakim of Judah decided to withhold the tribute payable to Nebuchadnezzar. It was useless for the clear-sighted prophet Jeremiah to rave and prophesy and repeat the century-old warnings of Micah and Isaiah, who also had clearly foreseen that Egypt was a crumbling power and that the vitality of the nations of the East, the peoples of the Euphrates and Tigris valleys, highly civilized, energetic, ambitious, and ruthlessly capable, was not to be withstood. Learning nothing from the fate of his predecessors, Jehoiakim persisted in his dream of Egypt's rejuvenation and in his folly defied the power of Babylon.

Though Egypt was no longer capable of aggression, she was still strong enough to repel an invader. Nebuchadnezzar failed to win a decisive victory against the armies of the Nile. But when he recoiled out of Egypt he gave the treacherous king of Judah short shrift. Jerusalem fell into panic on hearing of his approach. Entering the city without difficulty, Nebuchadnezzar had the rash and conceited Jehoiakim thrown from the walls, and made the son, Jehoiachin, king in his stead. Eventually the Babylonian gathered up from Judah all the citizens of any rank or worth, nobles and craftsmen, and carried them off to Mesopotamia.

As a result of successive deportations, there developed in the region of Babylon a considerable series of settlements of Jews, as they were called. The religious adventures of these displaced persons in their determined effort to maintain the worship of Yahweh in the face of the local god Marduk (Biblical Merodach) are related in the Book of Daniel, which covers the period from Nabopolassar to Cyrus.

On second thought, Nebuchadnezzar decided not to trust his puppet Jehoiachin and deposed him. A son of Josiah, Zedekiah, aged twenty-one, was set on the throne of Judah.

The last king of Judah in the direct line of David was almost a tragic figure, repeating the pitiful story of incompetence and defiance. He had changed his name from Mattaniah to Zedekiah to show his Babylonian conqueror that he was a new man and a loyal adherent. In fact, Zedekiah took a solemn oath of allegiance to Nebuchadnezzar. It was hardly a voluntary act. He had no other choice and, probably for that reason, felt quite at liberty to violate it whenever he saw fit. At any rate, the prophet Ezekiel assures us he was often foresworn.

Poor Zedekiah was not of tough fiber to stand firmly against the pressures exerted by the official riffraff and second-rate citizens

Nebuchadnezzar had left behind in Jerusalem. These wretches, feeling an overweening sense of importance in their position which only the absence of their betters had permitted them to fill, kept the weak-minded king under constant, nagging pressure to rely on Egypt and free himself of subservience to Babylon.

Zedekiah asked Jeremiah for advice and got more of it than he was able to cope with. Jeremiah was uncompromisingly insistent that Zedekiah stick to his bargain with the king of Babylon, which only seems to have aroused in Zedekiah a senseless defiance of both Jeremiah and Babylon. With guile, he sent an embassy to Nebuchadnezzar in Babylon carrying assurances of loyalty and submission. It is even reported that he went to Babylon in person, when summoned, to show his good faith. But he was a plaything of duplicity and intrigue. On his return to Jerusalem, he continued his irresponsible game of playing both ends against the middle, apparently quite oblivious of the fact that he, himself, was in the middle.

Outwardly at least, Zedekiah honored the mutual assistance pact he had signed with Nebuchadnezzar for eight years, but in the end the persuasions of the Egyptian ambassador at Jerusalem and the paid subversives among his courtiers proved too much for him. In spite of angry blasts from Jeremiah against the stupidity and suicidal folly of such a course of action, Zedekiah at last repudiated his pledge to Babylon and went wholly and openly over to Egypt.

In a fury, Nebuchadnezzar determined to end this gadfly nuisance and put the troublesome little kingdom of Judah and its pliable king in their political places. In 588 he sent his army on a rampage through Judah, pillaging and destroying as it went. One fortified city after another was stormed and taken; a year later only Azekah, Lachish, and Jerusalem remained.

Azekah was a very ancient stronghold that had been occupied even before the Israelites entered Canaan in the time of Joshua.

Now those who guarded the walls of Lachish a short distance to the southwest watched anxiously for signals from their beleaguered neighbor. The signals ceased. A concentrated attack on Lachish was not long delayed.

Lachish, some thirty miles southwest of Jerusalem, was also about fifteen hundred feet lower. It overlooked the Shephelah to the westward and protected the approaches to the mountain capital of Judah. It was very formidable, standing on a high hill behind double walls with many towers. The road leading to the gates in the outer wall led uphill under commanding battlements. Between the inner and outer gates ran a long rectangular walled court which was a death trap for any enemy trying to force an entrance that way. Lachish also was very old, having belonged to the Amorites in the time of Joshua. Nebuchadnezzar had destroyed it in 598 but although it had been rebuilt stronger than before, eleven years later it was unable to withstand a besieging technique that overwhelmed it once again. With its fall, Nebuchadnezzar was able to direct his entire attention to the taking of Jerusalem and its foresworn king.

Egypt did not stand idly by while its buffer ally slowly weakened under furious assaults, but sent an army to help Zedekiah. The Babylonians broke off the siege of Jerusalem and turned to meet approaching Egypt. The battle was bitter and brief. Egypt was defeated and driven back into the Nile valley.

Even though Jeremiah had foretold all this, when he went on to prophesy that if Zedekiah persisted in his defiance of Nebuchadnezzar he would meet the king of Babylon face to face and be carried away captive, the king and many of his courtiers refused to believe him. They pointed instead to the prophecy of Ezekiel which said that Zedekiah would never see Babylon. This apparent contradiction between the prophets brought confusion among those who assumed in their pride they could easily understand the words and ways of God. Only the common people were able to believe Jeremiah.

When Jeremiah in disgust decided to return to his own country, which was Anathoth in Benjamin, he was intercepted and
dragged before Zedekiah, charged with desertion and thrown
into prison in an attempt to placate the Egyptian faction at court,
which wanted to see him killed. This, however, Zedekiah was unwilling to do, probably out of fear of the people.

The actual business of besieging Jerusalem was undertaken by
five generals of Nebuchadnezzar who had set up his imperial
headquarters in Syria at Riblah on the Orontes River. The struggle
for the citadel of Judah continued month after month, passing
into a second year. Conditions of famine and disease were in-
describable. In vain Jeremiah promised that if the city were
opened to the Babylonians the Temple would not be destroyed
and the city, the houses, and the people would be spared. He
warned that the alternative was complete calamity. He seemed
to speak with authority; if not with the assurance of some secret
emissary of the enemy, then at least with the knowledge of
Yahweh. Nevertheless, resistance continued.

The Babylonians laboriously built many great banks of dirt all
around the city walls and on these banks erected high towers
from the tops of which they could repulse the defenders on the
walls with flights of arrows, while other attackers sapped and
battered sections of the walls below.

During these bitter, hungry days and nights, the Judaeans also
were desperately resourceful and determined. With catapults and
boulders they sent the towers crashing to the ground, poured
fire on the heads of those who ventured too close and counter-
mined the sappers who tried to burrow under the great walls.
The siege settled down to a contest of wits and ingenuity.

At length famine and disease did the work of a second army,
killing the defenders from within as the attackers wore them

down from without. After an incredibly stubborn defense lasting eighteen months, the end came suddenly in the middle of the night in August, 586 B.C. An entrance was made on the Temple side of the city, very possibly through the water tunnel under the walls south of the Temple enclosure. As the generals of Babylon entered the Temple sanctuary, the royal family with a few of the palace staff and servants fled the city through a fortified drainage ditch and so escaped out into the desert.

When they could not be found within the walls, they were pursued at daybreak and overtaken near Jericho. The royal party dispersed, every man for himself, but Zedekiah and his sons were taken alive and brought before King Nebuchadnezzar at Riblah as Jeremiah had foretold. There the king of Judah was accused of perfidious betrayal, of breaking his oath of allegiance and attacking the king who had given him back his kingdom. For this personal betrayal he was personally punished. He was forced to watch his sons being killed before his eyes. Immediately afterward his eyes were put out. Blind and bound, Zedekiah was carried off to Babylon which, as Ezekiel had foretold, he would never see.

And so the twenty-first king of Judah after David was overthrown. His royal house had reigned for over five hundred years. The high priest and rulers of the Temple were also brought before Nebuchadnezzar and had their heads cut off, all excepting the son of the high priest and a descendant of Zadoc who had been high priest in Solomon's time. He was carried away into captivity with the blind king.

Nor was this all. The king of Babylon sent his general Nebuzaradan to pillage the Temple of all its riches, even including the ceremonial utensils dating back to the time of Solomon, and to burn it, and to burn the royal palace and the entire city and to level the mighty walls of the city to the ground.

Then, with the great city lying in ruins and the last sanctuary of the amphictyony of Yahweh a heap of rubble, what was left of Jerusalem's defenders—fifty thousand of them, only the farmers and vinedressers being left behind—were driven like cattle, in midsummer heat, the full six hundred miles to Babylon and settled in places that are still unknown except for the congregation on the Chebar, an irrigation canal near the city of Nippur south of Babylon.

But even though the direct line from David had been extinguished, members of that house still lived, and the high priests from the Temple of Solomon were still represented by the descendants of Zadoc. The prophet Ezekiel too went into exile so that the word of the Lord would be available for the encouragement and comfort of the captive children of Israel. Even without their Temple and ancient sacrifice, the worship of Yahweh need not come to an end. It might undergo change but it could survive and grow.

XV

THE CAPTIVITY

THE DESTRUCTION of the Temple at Jerusalem did not mean the destruction of Yahweh, but it is obvious that a Lord God of Battles can mean little to a people living in captivity. And by the same token, a Lord of Battles without an army is without employment.

Moreover, the dazzling splendor of Babylon during the Chaldaean period far excelled the later glories of Athens and Rome, to say nothing of the glories of Jerusalem at any time. A people uprooted from craggy hills and dry mountains and deported to a civilization luxuriating in a land between two great rivers with a network of canals in a prospect as flat as a savannah, must undergo a change. And so inevitably their concept of their God must also change if, far from His leveled Temple and without the customary sacrifices, He is to inspire them to remain loyal and steadfast against the blandishments of the conqueror's God—especially one so awesome and apparently so powerful as victorious Marduk high on his towering ziggurat in Babylon.

A way had been already prepared by Micah and Isaiah for a transition from the thunderous, frightening God of Wrath who shook Sinai, into a concept more comforting and encouraging. The new and present need found new adaptable prophets.

Daniel, a member of Zedekiah's family, had been selected by his conquerors to be trained to serve the Babylonian empire. He was given the Chaldaean name of Belteshazzar. Three other Jews were chosen for the same purpose, whose names were changed to Shadrach, Meshach, and Abednego. All four became as learned as the principal Chaldaeans themselves and consequently, no doubt, acquired envious enemies.

Daniel, with his example of courage and of steadfastness to the Levitical law against the rewards and allurements of a successful pagan deity, helped to starch the will of his displaced and dismayed people, while at the same time his political sagacity and flair for the dramatic raised their prestige among their captors.

Now, too, there were no longer twelve tribes of Israel but only one—the tribe of Judah together with a few Benjaminites—and so about this time the Israelites came to be known commonly as Jews, a sort of nickname for Judaeans. But it had been within their tribal portion that the Temple of Yahweh had stood, and the unity that had existed between church and state strengthened their burning desire to return to their homeland far from the domination of the abominable, lecherous, mystical Marduk. Surely in time their own God would deliver them out of captivity and tribal humiliation.

At first, as they gathered in worship in a foreign land far from Jerusalem which they could hardly hope to see again in their own lifetime, their despair must have been very black. To bring them relief the prophet Ezekiel rose to inspired heights, turning their thoughts away from the predicament of their captivity towards a quite new and different prospect.

In the early days, Ezekiel sternly told the Jews that Judah was being punished not for rebelling against Babylon, but for rebelling against God, for idolatry and spurning His Word. Then, as the prophet saw and was moved by the depths of the people's misery, there came a change. "They that escaped" the death and destruction of Jerusalem, he said, shall mourn "every one for his in-iquity."

This was a new concept. Previously, the people had thought they suffered because of the transgressions of their king. And to the new idea of individual responsibility for Israel, Ezekiel added that some shall be saved through repentance. As this teaching found acceptance and took effect, he prophesied that Israel should be restored—and of course Israel was now Judah.

The amphictyony became no longer a league of tribes, but a union of individuals.

So the old relationship between Yahweh and the Jews as a tribal people, with reward or punishment following tribal be-havior, was modified and evolutionized into a new concept. Henceforth the relationship was to be very personal—not as it had been in the days of Abraham, for he was the head of a tribe and acted and spoke for his people—but on an individual basis even down to the least of them. Each Jew was now himself a temple of God, personally responsible to God for his own personal behavior.

In captivity the Jews were discovering the need for a God of mercy. An idea they formerly had repudiated when brought to them in their proud days by Micah and Isaiah, they now in their vale of tears accepted joyfully from Ezekiel. Now they could welcome this more personal concept of God, of which they had felt no need in the stark old days when they were a migrating host confronted by only one single communal necessity—survival. It was well that they could, for a spiritual rebirth was required to prepare them to take their place again in the international scheme of things that was reshaping all around them in the valleys of the Tigris and Euphrates.

In several respects the Jews did not have as hard a life in cap-tivity as in their own land, for the climate was mild and the earth fertile and well watered. They lived in villages around the city of Nippur between the two rivers, Tigris and Euphrates, about sixty miles southeast of Babylon. It was not at all like the captivity in Egypt. Here they had considerable freedom, and intermarriage was not at all unusual.

During their captivity near the capital of a great empire, the Jews became acquainted with coinage and the commercial methods of their captors, and learned the complexities of banking. They acquired property and accumulated money. They even adopted some of the religious embellishments of the Persians, such as angels and demons.

The magnificence and grandeur of Babylon itself could hardly fail to make an indelible impression on the Jews, for the city was one of the wonders of the ancient world, with its double rows of massive walls so wide that chariots could drive abreast along the top. Everything was colossal, to match the ambitions of its rulers. In the center of a government complex that included a towering palace with gardens hanging in terraces from roof to roof, was the lofty ziggurat, the towering temple once called in the Bible, Babel. The gardens and baths and fountains were supplied by water lifted from subterranean cisterns by devices operated by the endless tread of the feet of hundreds of slaves. The scale and scope of the fortifications and the standard of gracious living inescapably became a part of the thinking of those Jews who were born and matured in Mesopotamia.

It is extraordinary that the Jews did not succumb entirely to the appeal of the sophisticated civilization surrounding them. Some did, of course, but most of them, under the political leadership of Daniel and strengthened by the solacing and exciting new hopes inspired by Ezekiel, never wavered from devotion to their one true God.

To return to the political side of the story, Nebuzaradan, the Babylonian general who had been victorious at Jerusalem, chose

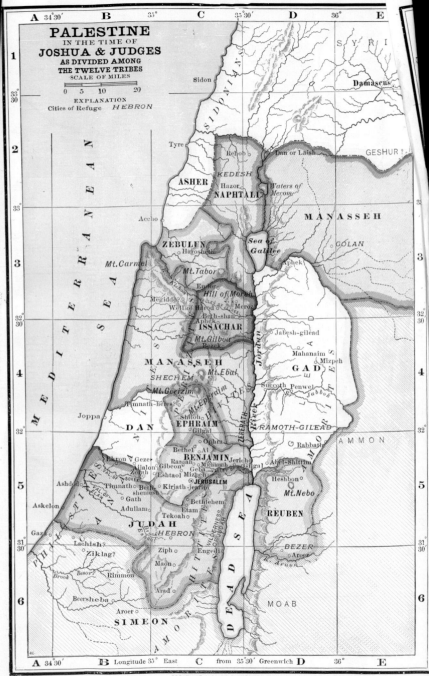

PALESTINE
IN THE TIME OF
JOSHUA & JUDGES
AS DIVIDED AMONG
THE TWELVE TRIBES
SCALE OF MILES

0   5   10   20

EXPLANATION
Cities of Refuge   *HEBRON*

SYRIA

Sidon

Damascus

Tyre   Rehob   Dan or Laish   GESHUR ?

KEDESH

ASHER   Hazor   Waters of
NAPHTALI   Meroms

Accho   MANASSEH

ZEBULUN   Sea of   GOLAN
Harosheth   Galilee

Mt. Carmel   Mt. Tabor   Aphek

Endor   Hill of Moreh
Megiddo   Merom
Well of Harod   Beth-shan
Aphek

ISSACHAR   Jabesh-gilead

Mt. Gilboa   Mahanaim   Mizpeh
Bezek   GAD

MANASSEH   Succoth Penuel

SHECHEM   Mt. Ebal
Mt. Gerizim

Timnath-heres   Shiloh
Joppa   Gilgal   RAMOTH-GILEAD

DAN   EPHRAIM   Rabbath
Gilgal   AMMON

Ophrah
Bethel   Ai

Ekron   Gezer   BENJAMIN   Jericho
Ramah   Michmash   Gilgal   Abel-Shittim
Aijalon   Gibeon   Geba   Mizpeh
Zorah   Eshtaol
Ashdod   Timnath   Beth-   JERUSALEM   Heshbon
shemesh   Kirjath-jearim
Gath   Bethlehem   Mt. Nebo
Askelon   Adullam   Etam
Tekoah   REUBEN
Gaza   JUDAH
HEBRON

Lachish ?   Ziph   BEZER
Ziklag ?   Engedi
Maon   Aroer

Brook   Besor   Rimmon   Arad
Beersheba   MOAB
Aroer

SIMEON

MEDITERRANEAN SEA

DEAD SEA

JORDAN   River Jordan

MADIANITES

MOABITES

AMORITES

River Arnon

PHILISTINES   CANAANITES   HITTITES   WILDERNESS OF JUDAH

SIDONIANS

A 34° 30'   B 35°   C 35° 30'   D 36°   E

A 34° 30'   B Longitude 35° East   C from 35° 30' Greenwich   D 36°   E

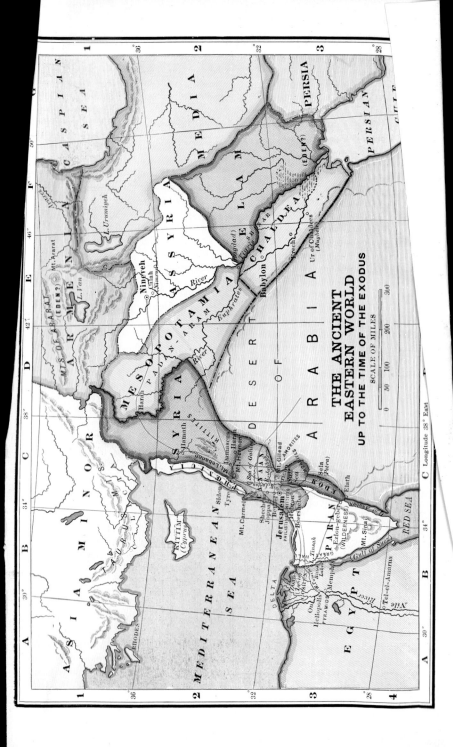

THE ANCIENT
EASTERN WORLD
UP TO THE TIME OF THE EXODUS

SCALE OF MILES

0   50   100   200   300

C   Longitude 38° East

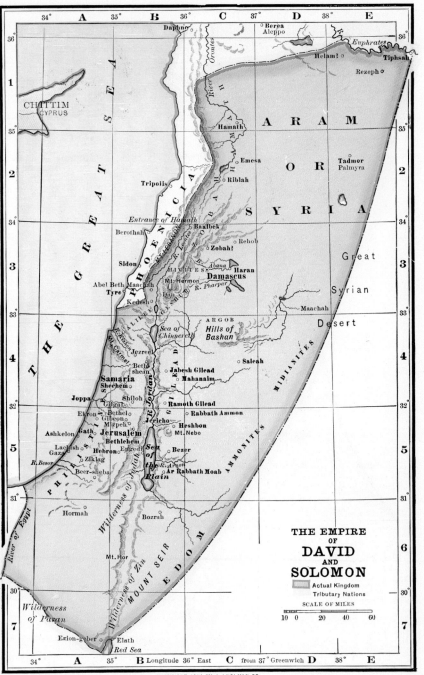

THE EMPIRE
OF
DAVID
AND
SOLOMON

Actual Kingdom
Tributary Nations

SCALE OF MILES

10 0   20   40   60

KINGDOMS
OF
JUDAH
AND
ISRAEL

SCALE OF MILES

0   10   20   30

THE ASSYRIAN AND BABYLONIAN POWERS

SCALE OF MILES

0   50   100   200   300

Yellow tint shows extent of Assyria proper.

Yellow outline shows Assyrian Power, at the time of Israel's deportation, 722 B. C.

Buff tint shows Israel at the time of deportation by Sargon, 722 B. C.

Red tint shows extent of Babylonia proper.

Red outline shows Babylonian Power, about 600 B. C.

Green tint shows Judah, carried to Babylonia by Nebuchadnezzar, 587 B. C.

CASPIAN SEA

MEDIA

SUSIANA

BABYLONIA

CHALDÆA

ARABIA

ELAM

PERSIA

PERSIAN GULF

Ecbatana (Achmetha)

Ragae

Aspadana (Gabae)

Bagistana

Susa (Shushan)

Charax (Spasini)

Pasitigris

Nippur

Erech

Ur

Ellasar (Larsa)

Nekub (Nagitu)

Babylon (Babel)

Borsippa

Sepharvaim

Cutha

Sea of Nedu

Accad

Sittace

Dura

MEDIA

M T S.

MTS.

Chuboras

MENTIANI

L. Arsene (L. Van)

Armenia (Van)

ARMENIA

Mt. Ararat

Euphrates

Cyrus

Araxes

Amida (Diarbekir)

Tigris

Lycus

ASSYRIA (ASSHUR)

Nineveh

Calah (Asshur)

Assur (Asshur)

Resen

Kalkhi

Dur-Sharrukin

Zab

Great Zab

Little Zab

Physcus

Sittace

ZAGROS MTS.

Tabriz

L. Montiquus (Urumiah L.)

L. Spauta (Salt Lake)

Mt. Orontes

Baghdad

MESOPOTAMIA

Nisibis

Singara

Edessa

Haran

Resaena

PADAN-ARAM

Tiplsah

Rezpeh

ARAM-NAHARAIM

Anatho

Tadmor (Palmyra)

Rehoboth

Circesium

Euphrates

Syrian Desert

TAURUS MTS.

CILICIA

CYPRUS (Kittim)

MEDITERRANEAN SEA (THE GREAT SEA)

Halys

Carchemish

Berea (Aleppo)

Antioch (Daphne)

Riblah

Kadesh

Hamath

Orontes

ARAM

PHŒNICIA

Arvad

Tripolis

Gebal

Byblos

Sidon

Zarephath

Tyre

Accho

Dor

Mt. Carmel

LEBANON

MT. LEBANON

Mt. Hermon

Damascus

ARGOB

BASHAN

Bozrah

Jabesh Gilead

Ramoth Gilead

Rabbath Ammon

Rabbath Moab

Dead Sea

Sea of Chinnereth

Jordan

Jabbok

GILEAD

ISRAEL

JUDAH

Samaria

Shechem

Shiloh

Joppa

Jerusalem

Jericho

Gaza

Bethlehem

Hebron

Beersheba

Elath

Gulf of Akabah

Red Sea

Ezion-geber

SINAI PENINSULA

Mt. Hor (or Tradition)

Desert of Paran

COPYRIGHT 1914 BY A. J. HOLMAN CO.

A   B   C   D   E   F   G   H   I   J   K

32° 34° 36° 38° 40° 42° 44° 46° 48° 50° 52°

D 40° Longitude E 42° East F from 44° G Greenwich 46°

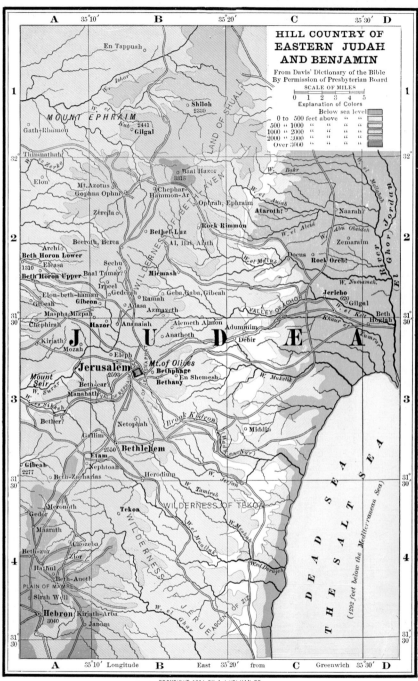

HILL COUNTRY OF EASTERN JUDAH AND BENJAMIN

From Davis' Dictionary of the Bible
By Permission of Presbyterian Board

SCALE OF MILES

0 1 2 3 4 5

Explanation of Colors

Below sea level

0 to 500 feet above " " "
500 " 1000 " " " "
1000 " 2000 " " " "
2000 " 3000 " " " "
Over 3000 " " " "

A   35°10'   B   35°20'   C   35°30'   D

En Tappuah

Ishar

W. el Zerka

MOUNT EPHRAIM

Gath-Rimmon

Kub 2441 Gilgal

Shiloh
2330

LAND OF SHUAL

1

Thimnathah

Baal Hazer
3316

W. el Bakr

W. et Meidah

W. el Ghor Jordan

32°

Elon

Mt.Azotus
Gophna Ophni

Chephar-Hammon-Ar

Ophrah, Ephraim

W. el Auiah

Ataroth?

Naarah?

Zérela

Bethel-Luz

Rock Rimmon

W. el Abed

W. Abu Obeideh

Zemaraim

River El Ghor Jordan

2

Beeroth, Berea

Ai, Hai, Aiath

W. el Maluk

Docus

Rock Oreb

Archi
Beth Horon Lower
1310 Eleasa
Beth Horon Upper Baal Tamar?

Sechu

Micmash

Irpeel

Gederah

Geba, Gaba, Gibeah

VALLEY OF ACHOR

W. Nueiameh

Jericho
620 Gilgal

W. el Kelt

Beth Hoglah

31° 30'

Elon-beth-hanan
Gibeah Gibeon
Maspha, Mizpah
Chephirah Hazor

Ramah
Ajasa
Azmaveth
Ananaiah

Alemeth Almon

Adummim

Khaur el

Aumran

31° 30'

Kiriath
Mozah

Anathoth

Debir

J   U   D   Æ   A

Eleph

Mount Seir
W. Surar

Jerusalem
2593
Beth-cara
Manahath

Mt.of Olives
Bethphage
Bethany
En Shemesh

W. es Sikkeh

VAL. of REPHAIM

W. Mukelik

3

Bether?

Netophah

Brook Kidron

Wady es Nar

Middin

31° 30'

Gallim

Etam 2550 Bethlehem

Gibeah
2277 Beth-Zacharias

Nephtoah

Herodium

W. Jerfan

W. Tamireh

WILDERNESS OF TEKOA

DEAD SEA

THE SALT SEA

(1292 feet below the Mediterranean Sea)

Meronoth
Gedor

Tekoa

W. el Muallak

W. Mubbah

W. es Sikkeh

4

Maarath

Beth-zur
Zior

Chozeba

Wad Derajeh

Hathul
Beth-Anoth
PLAIN OF MAMRE
Sirah Well

Hebron
3040 Kiriath-Arba
Janom

W. el Ghor

WILDERNESS OF JERUEL

ASCENT OF ZIZ

31° 30'

A   35°10' Longitude   B   East   35°20'   from   C   Greenwich   35°30'   D

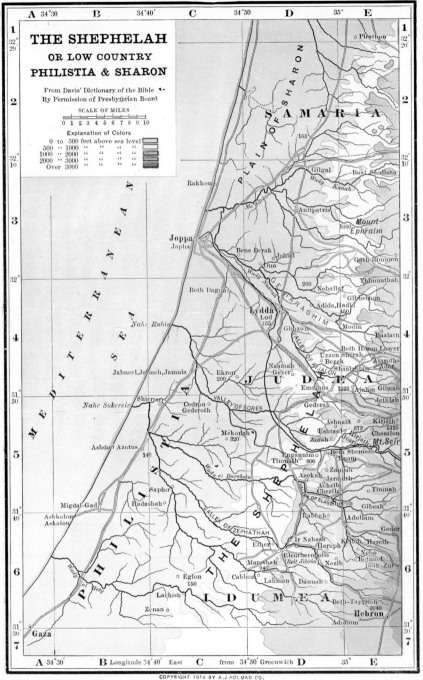

THE SHEPHELAH
OR LOW COUNTRY
PHILISTIA & SHARON

From Davis' Dictionary of the Bible
By Permission of Presbyterian Board

SCALE OF MILES
0 1 2 3 4 5 6 7 8 9 10

Explanation of Colors
0 to 500 feet above sea level
500 " 1000 " " " "
1000 " 2000 " " " "
2000 " 3000 " " " "
Over 3000 " " " "

PLAN OF JERUSALEM.

SCALE OF FEET

0   500   1000   1500

Green shows the Lowlands
Buff " " Highlands

Gedaliah, a member of a noble Judaean family, to be viceroy over the Jews left in Judaea. These were mostly farmers and vine-tenders and shepherds. Jeremiah was allowed to retire to Mizpah in Benjamin and more or less between the north and south kingdoms, and Baruch, his secretary, was also freed. The soil of Palestine was worked solely for the benefit of the Chaldaean empire at Babylon.

During the dislocation caused by the destruction of Jerusalem, Ishmael, one of the royal family of David, took refuge among the Ammonites and became consumed with the desire to replace Gedaliah as the resident head of Judah. Gedaliah was duly warned of this plot but was not able to believe it. His incredulity was fatal, for he was killed while having dinner with his guest Ishmael, who celebrated the occasion with a massacre of the Jews left in the city so ironically named Salem—peace.

The Jews who had been loyal to Gedaliah fled for their lives into Egypt, taking with them an unwilling Jeremiah and Baruch.

This disturbance so irritated Nebuchadnezzar that he sent a punitive expedition to discipline the Ammonites and Moabites and invade Egypt. The Pharaoh was slain and a puppet set up in his place and the Jews in Egypt were led off captive to Babylon to join their compatriots in exile lest worse befall them. This brought to an end the Hebrew nation as it had been for nearly seven centuries from the days of Joshua.

To keep the most fertile part of Palestine productive for Babylon, the Cutheans of the Medes and Persians were transported to settle in the central portion of the country and became known as Samaritans from the center of their settlement. Judah itself became a desert for seventy years and as for Jerusalem, Jeremiah summed it up with his lament, "How doth the city sit solitary, that was full of people."

But in spite of achieving tremendous power, the Chaldaean empire at Babylon was remarkably short lived. After the death of

Nebuchadnezzar a struggle for power brought Labosordacus to the throne. His son was Belshazzar. (The Bible calls him the son of Nebuchadnezzar.) It was when Belshazzar was impious enough to order the sacramental cups formerly in the service of the Temple at Jerusalem to be used at a feast, that the mysterious handwriting appeared on the wall, which only Daniel was able to interpret.

Meanwhile a new dynastic cataclysm was in the making. It began when Cyrus, son of Cambyses, succeeded to the throne of Persia in 559 B.C. Marching to the north of Persepolis and Shushan (Susa), Cyrus conquered the Medes and occupied their capital at Ecbatana. He then moved westward through the lands bordering on the Caspian and Black Seas, defeating Croesus at Pteria in 546 and going on to capture Sardis in Lydia in the same year. So while Babylon still ruled from the Tigris to the Nile, Cyrus had extended his authority from India to the Greek colonies on the Mediterranean, covering the Babylonian empire on the north like a vast blanket. Obviously a death struggle between the two great empires was not far off.

The inevitable happened. In 539 Cyrus defeated Babylon's army led by its crown prince Belshazzar (who had been weighed in the balance and found wanting) and took over the Chaldaean empire as far as Egypt. In 530, Cambyses II, the son of Cyrus, invaded and conquered Egypt so that the Persian empire finally extended from India to Cyrene in Africa and became the greatest empire ever known on earth up to that time.

XVI

RETURN AND REARMAMENT

WITH THE VICTORY of King Cyrus of Persia over the Chaldaean empire, a theory of government was put into operation, very different from the Babylonian. The Persians were a highly civilized people and Cyrus himself was liberal and enlightened and had a genius for government. His policy reversed that of the Assyrians, Babylonians, and Chaldaeans. Instead of deporting peoples, he set about restoring them to their homelands if they wanted to return. He divided his empire into large geographical units called satrapies and over each he put a governor called a satrap. He tolerated all kinds of religions and only demanded that all people remain loyal to his government.

In the first year of the reign of Cyrus, the Jews were liberated and soon grew influential enough to persuade the king to let them rebuild their Temple at Jerusalem. For administrative purposes, Cyrus created a small province, naming it Judah (Yehud in Hebrew) in the fifth satrapy which had its headquarters in Damascus. It was a modest little province, especially when compared with the old Judah, for it extended only from Bethel south to Beth-zur, a distance of about twenty-five miles. Even Lachish was occupied by the Edomites. But the new territory was deemed sufficient for the prestige of administering a shrine and supporting its staff.

When a migration of the Jews was announced, families entered their names to be among the first to return. Others gave donations towards buying materials and hiring skilled labor. The response was so impressive that Cyrus honored it by ordering the release and restoration of all the gold and silver utensils and ornaments raped from the Temple by the Chaldaean Nebuchadnezzar, even including the vessels of gold and silver that had been requisitioned for the service of Marduk.

Zerubbabel, grandson of King Jehoiachin of Judah, was chosen to lead the expedition, while the high priest Jeshua (a later spelling of Joshua) was not only the religious head of the returning congregation but was to be the supreme authority in Jerusalem. This was something new, for previously the supreme authority over Jerusalem had been the political head of the amphictyony. In addition to craftsmen, a large congregation of Levites who would serve the Temple as musicians, porters, police and so forth, were enrolled; among the laymen were Nehemiah and Mordecai and the prophets Haggai and Zechariah. Altogether those who were to be repatriated numbered forty-two thousand three hundred and sixty with seven thousand three hundred and thirty-seven servants including two hundred singing men and women. With them, for portage, went seven hundred and thirty-six horses, two hundred and forty-five mules, four hundred and thirty-five camels, and six thousand seven hundred and twenty asses.

This host set forth from Mesopotamia early in the reign of Cyrus and made the journey without incidents worth recording except that the people had to defend themselves occasionally against robbers, for their cavalcade was very tempting to poor desert nomads. It was a great mass migration like that of Abraham and Moses but, unlike theirs, this was a licensed invasion of the land.

Arriving amid the ruins of Jerusalem, Jeshua first built an altar on the site of the one that formerly stood in the Temple of

Solomon; as soon as it was finished, sacrifices were offered to the accompaniment of ecstatic rejoicing. As it was about the seventh month of the year and the autumnal equinox was at hand and the rainy season about to begin, the Feast of the Tabernacles marking the grape and olive harvest was celebrated soon afterward by the light of the full harvest moon.

As in Solomon's time, skilled labor was hired from Sidon and Tyre and, when the wild winter storms had subsided, cedars of Lebanon were lashed together in rafts and floated down the seacoast to Joppa. These transactions, which were based on grants and decrees from Cyrus, took time to negotiate but at last, after two years of preparation, the materials were ready and delivered at Jerusalem.

Then Zerubbabel and Jeshua assembled together all those over twenty years old and, with trumpets and cymbals, joyfully shouted praises to God with tears of released tension, and went to work.

But all was not a happy clashing of cymbals and psalm singing. The neighboring peoples surrounding the little province watched this reconstruction with jaundiced eyes. The Syrians and Samaritans soon petitioned Cyrus's successor, Cambyses, in protest against the re-establishment of a Jewish province in the midst of their satrapy. They complained that the Jews were laying the foundations of a rebellious city and that the Temple would in reality be nothing less than a citadel, as it had been before. They blocked the work as effectively as they could. Cambyses listened sympathetically to their pleas and withdrew the royal favor from the Temple project. The Jews suffered a period of distress and persecution at the hands of their neighbors, which reached serious proportions and seemed likely to spread throughout the whole empire. Work stopped until the second year of the reign of King Darius I the Great, who came to the throne in 522 B.C.

Darius returned to the policy of Cyrus and decreed that work on the Temple should proceed. At once new complaints were launched by the Samaritans and Syrians and other peoples roundabout, but Darius found and republished the original decrees of Cyrus and the work went on.

According to Cyrus's decrees the foundations of the Temple were to be made strong and the main chamber was specified to be sixty cubits wide and sixty cubits high. A cubit was measured by the length from a man's elbow to the tip of his middle finger, a fraction less than one and a half feet. Darius went even further. He decreed that all creatures and produce required for sacrifices must be supplied by the Samaritans and Syrians. Penalties for failing to do this were severe. For example, whosoever disobeyed, his house would be pulled down and made into a gibbet on which he must hang.

In the sixth year of the reign of Darius, after seven years of labor, the Temple was finished and the event celebrated with loud fanfares and huge sacrifices. This meant a great feast, for the meat of the sacrifices slaughtered by the priests was sold to the people for food. Of course, the new Temple was not so rich and magnificent as Solomon's had been, but few were alive who remembered that greater glory.

The noise and commotion of the celebration attracted all the Samaritans and Arabs within earshot. They ran to see what was happening and wanted to join in the fun, but were refused participation as unworthy. Such exclusiveness angered them and they retaliated by turning to Syria for help in hindering any further development of Jerusalem as a fortified place that was apparently unfriendly to them.

At one point the obstructionist tactics of the Samaritans and their allies grew so troublesome that Zerubbabel led a delegation back to Darius to complain. He won the royal support and Darius renewed his order that everything needed for the sacrifices must be supplied by the Samaritans and neighboring Syrians and Persians; he also added many valuable tax exemptions in favor of the Jews. But in spite of this the reconstruction work dragged on into another reign.

King Xerxes (Ahasuerus) followed his father Darius's policy of friendly support of the Jews in their restoration work and their efforts to rebuild not only the city but also the prestige of Jerusalem. However, the work had stalled so seriously that the priest Ezra (Esdras) sent a call throughout Persia to organize a new migration. The trip overland took more than four months, during the seventh year of Xerxes, the year after he had defeated Leonidas and his Spartans at Thermopylae and then sacked Athens.

On his arrival at Jerusalem, Ezra found a new problem. From a priestly point of view, conditions were deplorable and he loudly deplored them. Now that the Temple services had been restored, they were supposed to be properly performed according to the old Levitical priestly code. They were not. Ezra discovered great slackness and, to his dismay, sinful deviations from the prescriptions for purity. Many of the Jews had intermarried with Canaanites, Hittites, Zebusites, Ammonites, Moabites, Egyptians, and Amorites, which could not be tolerated in those who worshipped in the Temple of the Lord God. Even the sons of the high priest Jeshua had married outside the traditional people of the old amphictyony.

The purity of worship must be restored, so Ezra called on all the impure Jews to hold aloof from their foreign wives and put them away, even including the children of such marriages. Only in this way, he said, could the relapsed Jews be purified and return whole to their own people again. This measure met with popular support and his orders were carried out to the letter. It was an important decision with far-reaching consequences; at that late date it reaffirmed the exclusiveness of the Jews, which has been the source of many of their troubles as well as assurance of their survival.

After the Temple chamber was finished, the surrounding cloisters were built and Passover was celebrated there that spring, the Jews coming in from all the surrounding villages to participate in the festival. Then Ezra assembled all the people at the East Gate of the Temple and read to them the laws and injunctions of Moses.

With the rise of the new Temple, the chief power over the Jewish people in Judah had passed from the royal dynasty to the priesthood. Henceforth, the struggle for power between the secular rulers and the family of the high priest of the Temple would seesaw from one to the other for centuries. The church and state contest for power was destined to be contagious and later bedeviled Christendom for a thousand years.

Though Jerusalem was at last restored as a shrine, the city was still without walls and defenseless. Its houses, streets, and people were exposed to their enemies. Until the fortifications were rebuilt and strongly garrisoned, no treasure could be accumulated in the Temple. Even private property had to be safeguarded from surrounding hostile peoples, such as the Syrians, Arabs, and Samaritans.

The next Persian king, Artaxerxes, continued the policy of his father but carried it further. To him it seemed evident that it was unwise to have Jerusalem established solely as a shrine administered by a high priest. The Temple enclosure was designed to accommodate worshippers undisturbed by outsiders, but the Temple staff, priesthood, and others had to live in a city without walls, at the mercy of robbers, marauders, and other villains. Jews were beaten, robbed, even killed in the streets and environs of Jerusalem with startling frequency. They were often seized and dragged away into slavery. The king decided a strong layman was needed to administer the city.

At this time Nehemiah, a wealthy patriotic Jew, was living in Shushan (Susa) in Persia. One day in the ninth month (November-December) he happened to meet a friend in the palace and certain strangers from Judah who were talking about the pitiful state of affairs in Jerusalem and how the Jews were exposed to their enemies in the defenseless city. Nehemiah questioned them about conditions in Judah since he had last seen it. They told him that although the Temple had been rebuilt, the walls of the city still lay in rubbled ruins and the gates still gaped open through the charred debris. The people were at the mercy of their enemies.

Nehemiah was a man of considerable ability and influence and had been honored by an appointment to serve as cupbearer to King Artaxerxes which brought him close to the fountainhead of power in the empire. One day in Nisan (March-April) while serving his imperial master, his usually cheerful countenance was clouded and the king, noticing this, asked the reason for it.

Nehemiah told him that he had recently heard of the sorrowful plight of his countrymen in defenseless Jerusalem and how the value of the restoration of the shrine had been impaired, since the people who worshipped there were being robbed, beaten, and murdered in the open streets, their children seized and sold into slavery by ruthless enemies who were their neighbors. Nehemiah boldly took the opportunity to petition the king for permission to rebuild the walls and restore the gates of the ancient guardian city of the worship of Yahweh.

The Persian king, in an amiable mood, granted permission to rebuild the defenses of the city. He appointed Nehemiah governor of the province to see that the work was properly carried out, and gave him a letter to Adeus, governor of Syria, Phoenicia, and Samaria, ordering the Persian authorities in that satrapy to cooperate fully and to supply all the necessary materials. Immediately on arriving at Jerusalem with an escort, Nehemiah first showed the letter to God in the Temple, by exposing it open on the altar, before he delivered it to Adeus. Then it was made public by proclamation to the whole people.

Nehemiah was a man of parts, both as an engineer and an organizer. For instance, some time later, noticing that the Levites were insufficiently provided for and that service in the Temple had been reduced to a perfunctory affair with a skeleton crew, he instituted sweeping reforms in collecting tithes; soon the proper service in the Temple was restored.

Immediately after his arrival at Jerusalem, Nehemiah went secretly around the outside of the walls of the city on a night inspection, riding as far as he could, and when the heaps of rubble made further mounted progress impossible, he made the rest of the survey on foot. Next day he called together all the nobles and family leaders of the people and reported to them what he had found and the conclusions he had come to. They agreed to undertake the rebuilding of the defenses of the city.

Nehemiah had shrewdly decided that the best course was to raise all parts of the walls simultaneously. He divided the spans of the walls and the gates among the people, as nearly as possible making each family responsible for work adjoining or opposite their houses. Nehemiah and his own household also took their appointed places in the reconstruction. A detailed roster and work-progress report, including the names of the groups and the sections of the wall they worked on, was meticulously kept and anyone curious about it can read it in the Book of Nehemiah.

Under Nehemiah's leadership, the people fell to work in a frenzy of patriotism. Groups came from as far away as Jericho to work on the walls. Nobody knows today exactly where the walls were, especially on the northern side; little excavation has been possible because of the many sacred buildings scattered around the city which is now holy not only to the Jews but to Christians and Mohammedans. They were probably five miles in circumference, with many towers and eight gates.

There was no loitering for there was no time to lose. At first when the Amorites, Arabs, and Samaritans saw what was going on, they laughed. They thought the Jews were preparing for an armed rebellion against the power of Persia. When they realized that the work had the approval of the king and was authorized by royal decree, laughter turned into grimmer and more menacing sounds and actions. The Ammonites, Moabites, and Samaritans organized night forays into the city. They sneaked through the piles of stone and rubble, and every morning the robbed and beaten and dead were found in the streets of the city or around the walls. Plots were even afoot to lure Nehemiah to some place where he could be assassinated.

This situation Nehemiah dealt with promptly. Every worker on the walls and gates was ordered to toil with his weapons beside him and to sleep in arms, fully clothed, at his place in the wall. Guards were posted night and day, one for every work party, who also took turns at the labor. Trumpeters were posted every five hundred feet to sound an alarm. There were no gaps in the defenses anywhere in the perimeter of the walls. In this way the raids and killings were brought to an end and the work went forward fast. In the incredible time of fifty-two days the walls were finished. Only the great gates remained to be hung, the timber for which was to be supplied from the king's forest; it was slow in arriving. Nevertheless the completion of the walls was celebrated with a great parade around the whole circumference of the defenses by the entire population of the city. It must have been marvelously exciting to walk around the top of those great walls built by the people themselves.

At last the gates of the city were hung and guards posted day and night on the walls. The city was shut in, the gates closed and barred at sundown and not opened "until the sun be hot." They were kept shut throughout all of the Sabbath and those who attempted to conduct business as usual outside the walls were threatened with arrest.

Once again the shrine of the Lord God of Israel was protected by the stronghold of Jerusalem, a monument to dedication and devotion. But a great price was paid for the special fervor that brought this about. The late Isaiah had proclaimed it was God's intention that He should be available to all mankind, that He was the Lord of all people in all the world. But in order to bring the people of Judah to the pitch of getting the defense work done before their enemies could prevent it, Nehemiah had had to revive the old feeling of exclusiveness in the Judaeans. Consequently a strong national feeling was stirred up. The people were roused to a pride and enthusiasm that drove them to make great personal sacrifices, but it also widened the breach between them and their neighbors.

With the building of the second Temple and the restoration of the walls of Jerusalem, the Jews were almost unconsciously imbued with a feeling of indestructibility, an inner conviction that if they were faithful to God and His commandments, they would endure forever.

XVII

THE STRUGGLE AGAINST HELLENISM

THE SCHOOLBOY NOTION that history is a series of dramatic performances with very definite boundaries and intermissions is probably due to the fact that many historical writers have thought they must end their books with some sort of finality. They divide histories, like the school day, into periods. This gives the impression that history is a succession of events complete in tidy packages, boxed, tied—and labeled.

It is my idea, shared by some, that history is in a state of constant change and flow from cause to effect which in turn evolves into another cause. History is for all practical purposes without end, and for that matter with no very definite beginning. It is a state of continual change but not necessarily continual progress. It is not even like a game between two sides in which one can keep score between "the goods" and "the bads" and announce from time to time which side is ahead and at the conclusion which side won.

While the people of Judah were preoccupied with rebuilding Jerusalem and its Temple, the Bible contains no hint of the great events taking place in the world about them that would eventually affect them decisively. Until the people of the many mythological gods came into direct conflict with the people of the one true God there was no involvement with them, and therefore no

Biblical mention of them.

The power of Persia under Darius met a check in its westward expansion when the Greeks defeated them at Marathon. The period of Greek expansion and colonization was about to begin. The inhabitants of the many Greek city states in Asia Minor were known as Hellenes and the commercial lingo they made popular and almost essential in international trade was called Koine.

The language of Judah was also changing. Hebrew was used almost exclusively by the priests and scholars, whereas the people spoke a more universal Semitic dialect called Aramaic. So Asia and the eastern part of the Mediterranean became bilingual to a considerable degree.

Even when Alexander appeared on the scene and, tramping fatefully across the most venerable cities and civilizations of the east, cried, "All men must become one people," the Jews, aloof in their mountain fastness far from the main routes of his marches, apparently heard no echo of it. If they had, it would have startled them into some attention, for it aimed at the heart of their precious exclusiveness. They were to hear it shouted to them in unmistakable terms before many Passovers.

With the rapid rise of Alexander of Macedonia, beginning in 336 B.C., there was no escaping the decisive nature of this ideological conflict, for in 334 Alexander entered Asia Minor and soon afterward won an important victory over the allies of Persia at the river Granicus. Passing through the Cilician Gates, he then decisively defeated Darius III at Issus in Cilicia.

Alexander did not pause after that; his object was to capture all the naval bases of Persia along the Mediterranean so that their fleet, bereft of harbors and allies, would fall easily into his hands. With incredible speed he marched south, subduing Syria, taking Damascus, Sidon, and finally Tyre, passed through Palestine and, overcoming a stubborn resistance at Gaza, entered Egypt and mounted the throne of the Pharaohs. He founded many cities in his own name but the most famous was the one at the mouth of the Nile that was to become a center of Hellenistic culture and attract a large Jewish population.

Alexander's only visit to Jerusalem was a personal one after the subjection of Gaza. He paid honor to the Temple Deity and its priests for in such matters his policy was like the Persians. Knowing the west was secure, Alexander turned east and conquered Persia to the Indus. In 323 B.C. he died.

An account of Alexander's meteoric career is given in the First Book of Maccabees, which was included in the Christian Bible until the Council of Trent (A.D. 1546) as part of the Apocrypha. The Council decided that the Apocrypha was not sufficiently canonical to include in the Bible. The Greek Church, however, decided it was canonical. The First Book of Maccabees is retained in the Roman Catholic (Douay) Bible. It was never a part of the Holy Scriptures of the Jews. Nevertheless the First Book of Maccabees is the best source for events in Jewish history from 175 to 135 B.C. and, for our non-canonical purpose, can be useful.

As a result of Alexander's short conquest Hellenistic culture became the prevailing one from Syracuse in Sicily to the Euphrates. It had many attractions, especially for the young and vigorous and the old and thoughtful. So the Jews broke into two bitter factions—those who succumbed to Hellenism and those who resisted it and remained apart from it. There was no avoiding the issue. It was a conflict without armament but not without weapons—the weapons were ideas.

After Alexander's death, the long, vicious, decimating wars began between his generals. Once again Judah was caught between the jaws of a vise, between Egypt and Syria. Ptolemy I, Soter, moved on them first, apparently in peace. The general came into Jerusalem on the Sabbath as though he intended to make sacrifice in the Temple. Suddenly he seized control of it, unopposed, for the Jews would not resist him with force of arms on their sacred day. They had no second chance. Many Jews and even Samaritans were deported into Egypt and settled at Alexandria. They made a good living and later some migrated there voluntarily, but even in exile the Jews sent annual sacrifices to the Temple at Jerusalem and the Samaritans to their shrine on Mount Gerizim.

Soter's son, Ptolemy II, Philadelphus (285–246 B.C.), had great respect for the Jews in Alexandria and gave them a quarter of the city near the palace. Later on, they were allowed to live anywhere without restrictions. He freed those of them his father had enslaved, by paying for their freedom, and since there were one hundred and twenty thousand Jews in Egypt, not including the children, this was an exceedingly handsome gesture of good will.

Ptolemy was busily assembling the great library of half a million books at Alexandria and, understanding that the Jews lived by their own law, he thought books of that law should be in the library and available to everyone. But most of the young Alexandrian Jews knew only Greek and consequently their own books were not open to them. At the suggestion of the librarian, Ptolemy decided that a strict and authentic translation should be made from the original Hebrew into Greek.

Being sincere in this purpose, he sent to Eleazar, the high priest of the Temple in Jerusalem, asking that the books of the law be sent to Alexandria together with a deputation of scholars deemed capable of making such a translation. Seventy-two wise men were chosen and later two more were added. With exchanges of gifts on both sides, the scholars were received in Alexandria and went to work. This was about the year 250 B.C. The resulting translation, the first the Bible had undergone, was of the Pentateuch, the first five books. The translation was called the Septuagint, which means seventy, in honor of the scholars who worked on it. In time other books of the Old Testament were similarly translated into Greek, making up the version that was later translated into Latin by St. Jerome and into English by John Wycliffe and, still later, by the King James commission which used the Hebrew for cross reference.

For a while the Jews lived in peace, left pretty much to themselves provided they were prompt in paying their taxes, as apparently they were, because they were even allowed to mint their own money.

But the superiority of the Ptolemys was partly based on the relative ineffectiveness of the Seleucids, and this situation was challenged by the first strong man among the latter, King Antiochus III the Great. Both dynasties were founded by generals of Alexander the Great, Ptolemy a Macedonian nobleman and Seleucus, king of Syria. Antiochus was determined to regain from Egypt the control of Palestine which had originally been allotted to his dynasty, and also Coeli-Syria, that goodly country lying between the Lebanon mountains and Mount Hermon. His first aggressive effort was defeated south of Gaza, but when the Egyptians began pushing north in the interests of their commerce, and especially their need for timber, he decisively defeated their army in 198 B.C. at the foot of Mount Hermon at the headwaters of the Jordan. Subsequently the Jews helped him drive the Egyptian garrison out of the citadel of Jerusalem.

As a reward, Antiochus III was generous to Jerusalem and granted the people of Judah considerable privileges and immunities, remitting taxes for three years and even subscribing to the embellishment of the Temple and contributing to the religious observances.

Murdered during an attempt to seize a temple treasure in the East, Antiochus was succeeded by his son Seleucus IV, Philopater, who also had an eager eye for temple treasure, this time the treasure at Jerusalem, but he was not successful in raiding it by a deputy. Mention is made of the attempt, though, in the Second

Book of Maccabees and Josephus, because it was the treasure of the Lord God.

With the accession of Antiochus IV Epiphanes, grandson of Antiochus the Great, the troubles of the Jews again intensified. The policy of forbearance against them was now entirely changed, for this Seleucid was brutal and ruthless. His policy was to rule one united people all under one law and government. He began by attacking Egypt, but the rise and spread of the power of Rome after Paulus defeated Perseus the Macedonian in 168 B.C., threw the shadow of the rising empire from the west across all Asia Minor and brought the Seleucid ravager to a full stop in Egypt. As he started home to defend himself, Rome was poised to fall upon the Hellenist colonies in Asia.

On his way back, Epiphanes entered Jerusalem by treason, some of his party opening the gates to him, and he put all to the sword in a ghastly holocaust. The sacred books were burned. He appointed high priests not of the high priestly line, he profaned the Temple with idols, stripped it bare of ornament and looted its treasury, thrust Hellenism on the Jews and tried to force them to violate the Mosaic law.

All the special laws and customs of the Jews were forbidden to them. There was not even to be any more circumcision lest it spoil the unity among the people, and when later his inspectors found the mothers were secretly circumcising their little sons, the children were strangled, their mothers crucified with their babies' bodies hanging around their necks. All those who resisted, or even objected, were killed to enforce submission to this new bloody concept of empire. Some submitted; many hid in remote caves in the ravines and wilderness as in olden times. It was a dark day for the people of the amphictyony of Yahweh. Never before had it been reduced to such impotence and paucity of numbers.

XVIII

JUDAS MACCABEUS AND

THE SELEUCIDS

THE BASIC IDEA behind the policy of Antiochus IV Epiphanes was
simply to place the people of his kingdom under a completely

uniform government. However, the attempt to end all at once and violently a religious cult and customs that were a hundred generations old, was bitterly resented and stubbornly resisted. At first no more than a scattered remnant of Jews held strictly to the old ways, but as the brutal suppressions grew more ferocious the resistance movement grew stronger and more determined, until the ground was saturated with blood and ready for the seeds of open armed rebellion. "There was very great wrath upon the People," we are told in First Maccabees.

Then, "in those days arose Mattathias, the son of John, the son of Simeon, a priest of the sons of Joarib, from Jerusalem, and he abode in the mountains of Modin," some miles west of Bethel. He was a descendant of Hasmon (or Hashmon), and so members of his family were called the Hasmonaeans.

This Mattathias had five sons, John, Simon, Judas who was called Maccabeus (the Hammerer), Eleazar, and Jonathan. "These saw the evils that were done in the people of Judah and in Jerusalem."

Probably because of the size and prestige of this family the military agent of Antiochus, escorted by Syrian troops, decided to make examples of them. He chose them to be the first to make pagan sacrifice in public. This was at Modin where Mattathias was a priest of Yahweh. Mattathias indignantly refused. When a Jew in the crowd came forward and tried to make the pagan sacrifice, Mattathias drew his sword and killed him. He also killed the military agent from Antiochus while his sons fell upon the detachment of Syrians, killing several. They then tore down the pagan altar.

Such defiance of the authority of the Seleucid dynasty was obviously not safe and the descendants of Hasmon did not linger to debate the holy righteousness of their actions. Before fleeing into the desert, leaving everything he possessed behind him, Mattathias lingered only long enough to say, "If anyone be zealous for the laws of his country and the worship of his God, let him follow me."

Entire families of the pious Hasidim sect did follow him. The refugees hid in caves and ravines in the hills north of Jerusalem, for Modin was on a road between Jerusalem and Joppa.

The Syrian commander at Jerusalem led out a force to hunt them down and finding some of them, tried to persuade them to give themselves up. But the Hasidim refused. So the Syrians waited until the Sabbath, a day on which they knew a devout Jew would not fight, and then burned them alive in the caves where they were hiding. About a thousand were killed in this way.

Some of these quixotic people escaped to join Mattathias whom they elected their leader. He told them they must fight on the Sabbath or become their own enemies. Anyone who wanted an easy slaughter would attack them on that day, in which case it would not be long before the whole nation would die without fighting and no one would be left alive to worship Yahweh.

Realizing the seriousness of the situation, Mattathias set about raising an army which was, of course, nothing more than a guerrilla force, and put it under the command of his aggressive son, Judas Maccabeus, the Hammerer. At first their principal operations were overthrowing pagan altars, killing any apostate Jews they could catch, and circumcising the boys. Within a year of his revolt at Modin, Mattathias was dead and Judas in complete command.

The disorders in Judaea spread until the government at Antioch was forced to look for a remedy, so an armed force was quickly sent to wipe out Judas and his rampaging little band. But the disciplinary force was not large enough, and Judas defeated it, killed the leader and took his sword for himself.

It reminds us again of the paradoxical observation that "small armies are defeated, large armies starve." For when the Seleucid power, now thoroughly roused, assembled a formidable host and again went after Judas and his guerrillas, the loosely organized Jews were not eager to join battle; they were too hungry. Judas turned this to advantage, preaching to them the holiness of their mission and almost surely throwing in a hint of the food and booty that lay before them. He roused them to such a pitch that they overwhelmed the soldiers, killed their general and put them to flight.

King Antiochus was beside himself with frustration and rage, somewhat garnished perhaps with fear. He now began gathering together his own personal army and added hired mercenaries, but when he saw how his expenses were mounting up, he decided to use this army to attack Persia instead, in order to collect tribute so he could afford what he had undertaken. He left his general Lysias in charge. Lysias understood the seriousness of the situation in the province of Judaea and mustered a strong force of forty thousand infantry and seven thousand cavalry, sending them south as far as Emmaus on the southern Jerusalem-Joppa road. Here another scattering of Syrian mercenaries and renegade Jews joined up with them.

Judas reconnoitered the Syrian position and accurately judged the formidable size of the army confronting him. After an impassioned oration to the Hasidim on the past glories of their people, he set them in the ancient order of battle that had given so many victories to their ancestors. Following the old custom of Moses, he dismissed all those who were newly married and sent away those who had recently come into new possessions, lest they might not fight desperately enough, hoping to live to enjoy their newly acquired property. For Judas let no one be under any illusions: this was a decisive moment. They would either gain or lose forever the right to worship Yahweh according to His laws as they had always done and wanted always to do. He ordered the entire host to make supplication to Yahweh, reminding them that they were His people and fought in defense of His worship. He then told them to be ready to fight at dawn.

The Syrians, however, had no mind to wait until the next day, but sent the general, Gorgias, with five thousand infantry and one thousand horses to fall upon the troops of Judas by night, using the renegade Hellenized Jews, familiar with the land, as guides.

The watchful and resourceful Judas saw what they were up to and set afoot a counterplan of his own. First, he calmly allowed his men to have a good meal. Then, leaving their campfires burning brightly, he drew them quietly off and took them overland through the night toward Emmaus.

When Gorgias reached the campfires sometime during the night and saw they were unattended, he decided the Jews must be hiding somewhere in the hills and wasted his time playing hide-and-seek with an opponent that was not there.

Shortly before daylight Judas appeared unexpectedly before the three thousand men stationed at Emmaus. The troops there were not the pick of the Syrian forces but the ill-armed discard, yet they were in a well-fortified position.

Telling his men that for Yahweh they should be willing to fight with their naked bodies, not well-armed as they were, he ordered the trumpets to sound an attack. Benefiting by the element of surprise, they overwhelmed the Syrian polyglots and chased them as far as Gadara, the plains of Idumaea and Ashdod. Very few, if any, of that three thousand survived.

Judas restrained his men from pursuing the quest for booty, since the main force with Gorgias must still be accounted for. Once that was defeated, no other opposition need be immediately expected and they could plunder to their hearts' content.

Gorgias, on his futile way back to Emmaus, saw the smoke of the burning camp from afar, the sight of which so dismayed his troops that they fled northward. Then, as though the enemy had been already defeated, Judas fell upon their baggage train and enriched his army to a considerable degree, for there was a great quantity of gold and silver as well as valuable purple and blue cloth. On the march back to headquarters the Jews sang hymns in praise of God to whom they attributed the victory.

Lysias was confounded by this defeat but by the following year he had assembled an army of sixty thousand men which, with five thousand cavalry, he led into the Judaean hills, pitching camp at Bethsura. Judas had with him now only ten thousand men, and when he saw the great host before him he prayed fervently for God to help him.

The army of Syria was so large it could not encamp or move as a complete unit in such rugged broken country, so Judas rushed at the first segment of it he encountered with all the fury he could muster, defeating it with a slaughter of five thousand.

Lysias was an eyewitness to the ferocity of the attack. Finally, he realized how determined the Jews were to gain the right to worship their own God in their own way under their own religious laws, and that they preferred death to failure. He withdrew the large remnant of his army to Antioch and began increasing its size with mercenaries.

Encouraged by his successes, Judas told the people they should go up to Jerusalem and purify the Temple and offer proper sacrifices there again. He led them there but found the Temple deserted, its gates burned down and weeds growing in the courts.

Sending a detachment of his soldiers to engage the attention of the Hellenized Syrians and Hellenized Jews who were walled up in the citadel, Judas went about the business of cleansing and purifying the Temple where the Syrians had sacrificed a pig on a Greek altar. Then Judas offered sacrifices to the Yahweh of old, the God of Joshua, Deborah, and Gideon, the Lord God of

Hosts and of Battles, on an altar newly built for the occasion. All the people carried lights and candles. This was the celebration that instituted Hanukkah, the Festival of Lights, on December 25, 165 B.C. Needless to say, there was very great rejoicing at the revival of the customs of Judah in the Temple of the ancient amphictyony. The pious Hasidim were satisfied and happy.

"Judas also built the walls round the city and reared towers of great height against the incursions of enemies and set guards therein." He also fortified the city of Bethsura just north of Hebron to serve as a citadel against any force attacking from Idumaea.

Impressed by the unyielding resolution of the Jews and the vast cost of trying to subject them, Lysias was at last willing to grant them the religious liberty they craved. It was too late. The Jews had been too successful and had suffered too many hardships to settle for less than complete political independence which they were determined to get. That, Lysias was equally determined to prevent. The war went on.

Judas, with his mobile guerrilla force, now moved rapidly about the country rescuing Jews who were being persecuted and butchered by the surrounding Semitic peoples. First he fought a war of deliverance against the descendants of Esau, the Edomites in Idumaea.

Realizing he could not be everywhere at once, though it must often have seemed to his enemies as though he were, Judas sent his brother Simon north into Galilee on a rescue mission, and taking his younger brother Jonathan with him, went over Jordan into Gilead. He left behind him in Judah a reserve under the command of two generals, the son of Zacharias and another, with orders not to attack but to stay on the defensive.

Once over Jordan, Judas first made peace with the Nabataeans (an Arab people) who gave him much valuable information about the state of affairs in Gilead. Then, moving with characteristic speed, he surprised his enemies near Besor and took the city, afterwards pressing on to a fortified place where the Jews had shut themselves up and were under siege. Coming up in the early morning when the besiegers were already on the scaling ladders, Judas threw his troops on them from the rear and scoured them off the walls, routing them and pursuing them with satisfactory slaughter—about eight thousand. His reputation for success soon caused his enemies to flee at the mere news of his approach.

Then at the Jabbok, Judas broke up a planned attack by anticipating the enemy and attacking first. He never seemed to fight two battles in the same way. Having killed and burned until there was no opposition of consequence left, he gathered in all the Jews he had liberated and escorted them back to Judaea where he could guard them better. With them also he took great arsenals of weapons and treasures of gold. One city on his homeward route was foolish enough to refuse passage through its walls. He attacked, and marched over the bodies of the dead. The Jewish historian, Josephus, tells us "not one of the Jews was slain in these battles"—on this we shall make no comment.

On learning of Simon's success in bottling up the Syrians in Ptolemais in Galilee and the clean sweep Judas was making in Gilead, Zacharias decided to bestir himself and win a reputation of his own. So he launched an attack on Gorgias with the result that he was badly beaten with a loss of two thousand, "Because he did not hearken to Judas and his brethren . . . was not of the seed of those men by whom salvation was brought to Israel."

On his return, Judas, now with better equipment and more money, never paused but pressed on to engage the Idumaeans, taking Hebron and Ashdod. Even Jerusalem called for his attention. In the citadel overlooking the Temple enclosure a group of "runagate" Jews (as Josephus called them) were still shut up and occasionally made sorties to raid the defenseless Jews who came to make sacrifices to Yahweh in the Temple. Judas decided to lay siege to the citadel and wipe out this pocket of resistance.

He had only commenced this operation when a distant event interfered with his plans. King Antiochus, having failed in his attack on a Persian stronghold where he expected to capture great treasure of gold, died of a stroke brought on by fury and frustration. Before he died he named his son Antiochus V, called Eupator, a boy of nine, his heir and his general, Philip, regent.

Philip was a long way off but Eupator was in Antioch with the Syrian general Lysias who acted promptly in his own interest. He marched down the coast, turned inland through Idumaea and, coming up from the south, intended to strike Judaea from the rear. He laid siege to Bethsura just north of Hebron as he entered the Judaean highlands.

Bethsura was without a food supply sufficient to endure a siege of any length because it was the fallow year, the one year in seven when the Jews let their lands lie idle and unproductive so the earth's fertility might be restored.

As soon as Judas got word of what Lysias was doing, he broke off the siege of the citadel in Jerusalem and marched south to meet his enemy. He did not take up a position behind the walls of any city, but pitched his camp opposite the Syrian. Judas wanted plenty of elbow room for his army; his tactics were most effective in open warfare where his sudden changes of direction and concentration of attack gave him an advantage.

The sight of the Syrian host, however, was enough to disconcert anyone, for they had paid Judas the compliment of bringing against him the mightiest force they could muster. They had with them their entire corps of elephants, each beast surrounded by a thousand men and five hundred horses. On each elephant's back was a great wooden tower full of archers.

True, this Syrian formation was designed for battle in wide-open, flat spaces and the broken, mountainous, ravine-scarred terrain of Judaea put it at a crowded disadvantage, but it was formidable nonetheless. Judas did what he could by ordering an attack.

One incident gives a fairly good idea of why the men of Judah were such dangerous enemies even in small numbers and even when fighting alone. "Eleazar, brother of Judas, saw one of the elephants was harnessed with the king's harness and it was higher then the other beasts and it seemed to him the king was on it. And he exposed himself to deliver his people and to get himself an everlasting name. He ran up to it boldly in the midst of the legion, killing on the right hand and on the left, and they fell by him on this side and that side. He went between the feet of the elephant and put himself under it and slew it and it fell to the ground upon him and he died there."

But in spite of the courage of Eleazar, the Jews would have been decisively defeated had not Judas managed to withdraw his army and get it behind the walls of Jerusalem.

Lysias then quickly took Bethsura, doing the inhabitants "no harm than sending them out naked," and then moved on to besiege Judas in Jerusalem which was also short of food and supplies. Soon famine stalked the city. It was a dark time for the Jews.

At this critical point word came to Lysias that the Seleucid regent, Philip, was returning from Persia with his army and was approaching Antioch, the Seleucid capital. Alarmed now for his own future, Lysias made a hasty treaty with Judas so that he could return northward and fight the regent for supremacy over the boy king Eupator.

He came to terms with Judas Maccabeus and entered Zion. Upon seeing the great strength of the fortifications, Lysias broke his word and ordered the walls thrown down, though subsequent events indicate that the order was not carried out completely.

The political division and rivalry for leadership among the

Syrians were a great boon to the Jews. The plot, or rather the plots, began not only to thicken to the point of opacity but moved with dizzying speed. Demetrius, a son of Antiochus IV, had been raised as a hostage in Rome, and while the Syrian generals fought to see who would dominate Antiochus V Eupator, Demetrius made his escape, landed on the seacoast of Syria, establishing himself at Tripoli, and claimed for himself the throne of the Seleucids.

The Syrian army took matters into its own hands and, seizing the persons of Eupator and Lysias, delivered them into the hands of Demetrius—after which they did not live long.

At the urging of groups of renegade Jews, Demetrius appointed Alcimus to be high priest of the Jews, an act which aroused bitter resentment among the Hasidim because Alcimus was not a member of the hereditary high priestly family. As soon as Alcimus was installed in his high office in the year 160 B.C. he set about slaughtering every devout orthodox Jew he could get his hands on. Judas Maccabeus, after a series of rescue raids along the seacoast, began trailing Alcimus about the country, evening matters up with a vengeance.

When Alcimus called on Demetrius for help, he sent Nicanor to bring this bloody struggle to an end if it could be done. Nicanor, a deceitful character, tried to lure Judas into a conference in order to assassinate him but the Maccabeus was too wise a fox and escaped the trap. Dropping all pretense, Nicanor forced Judas into battle and although it cost Nicanor five thousand men, Judas was compelled to take refuge behind the walls of Jerusalem. Nicanor then peremptorily served an ultimatum on the priests: if they did not surrender Judas to him he would pull down all Jerusalem.

Nicanor with his reinforced army of about nine thousand was at this time at Beth-horon, a city at the foot of the Judaean highlands between Jerusalem and Modin. Judas, sallying forth with

157

a small army of not more than three thousand, chose a position at Adasa which lay between Nicanor's position and Jerusalem, on the crest of the high ridge of the Judaean range. The ravines and narrow defiles favored the smaller force, but of the battle that followed we have no description, except only that when it was over Nicanor was not only defeated but dead. The Seleucid army threw away its arms and desperately tried to escape, but all the people in the countryside rose up and put on their armor and went out against the fugitives so that none of them survived.

Judas understood that his opposition to the full united power of the Seleucids would become increasingly difficult to sustain, and the success of the Roman-raised Demetrius drew his attention to the rapidly rising western power of Rome. He decided it would be of tremendous advantage to him if he could offer friendship to Rome and negotiate a treaty of mutual support. Therefore he sent two ambassadors, one of whom was Eleazar's son, to make a treaty of confederacy with the Roman Senate if they could. In this way Judas hoped he could protect his people by an alliance with religiously tolerant Rome against the hated Hellenistic Seleucids and their profane interference with the Temple worship.

The embassy was a success and the treaty was written on brass. It included a Roman "cease and desist" order against Demetrius.

But during the months while the embassy was on its mission, Demetrius sent a new army of twenty thousand into Judaea, under the command of Bacchides, which approached Jerusalem down the Jordan Valley and headed up into the highlands of Judah by way of Gilgal. Judas had with him only three thousand chosen troops and at the sight of the great Syrian host below them, his elite force quickly dwindled to a mere eight hundred. These tried to dissuade Judas from giving battle against such odds, but the Maccabeus would not listen to them.

Bacchides had drawn up his army in battle formation, with

cavalry on both wings and light infantry and archers in the center. He himself commanded the right wing.

Taking advantage of the terrain, Judas ordered his little band forward, concentrating on the right wing. The ferocious Jewish attack broke up the Syrian right and drove it back into the crevices of the rough ground behind it. But as the Jews followed up the rout, the Syrian left wing swept round and closed in behind them; Judas did not have enough men to keep it engaged while he finished off the routed force in front of him.

They fought it out, but it was in vain, and in this battle in 160 B.C. Judas Maccabeus was defeated and in the combat lost his life. Under a treaty of truce, his brothers Simon and Jonathan took his body away and buried it with his forefathers at Modin. John was assassinated soon after, Jonathan became high priest and ruler, while his older brother Simon commanded what was left of the army of Judah.

XIX

CIVIL WAR

THE ONE HUNDRED and sixty years between the death of Judas Maccabeus and the New Testament were turbulent and confusing almost beyond belief and understanding. The leaders of Syria, Judaea, and Egypt began an involvement that was little short of fantastic. They changed partners like couples in some kind of deadly country square dance.

As though the situations alone were not puzzling enough, the personalities compounded the confusion. There were more than one Antiochus, more than one Demetrius, a series of Ptolemys, and two Cleopatras. There was even another Alexander! Meanwhile Rome, hovering over the horizon, was beginning to prepare for invasion by intrigue and bribery.

One campaign throws some light on the tactics used by two of the leaders. The Seleucid king named Alexander, occupying Antioch, sent word to Jonathan Maccabeus, a young brother of Judas, not to "sit still among the mountains" but "come down into the plain" and fight.

Jonathan, who was favored over Simon by the Seleucids and had been offered a crown and purple raiment by both Syrian factions, took ten thousand of his best troops and, with his brother Simon, pitched camp outside the walls of Joppa which had shut its gates in his face. On second thought, however, they opened the gates again.

Alexander sent his general Apollonius with three thousand horse and eight thousand foot soldiers to Ashdod on the plain quite a distance to the south of Joppa against which he moved slowly. Jews were engaged on both sides of this conflict, for the Syrians from time to time enlisted many disaffected or Hellenized Jews as mercenaries.

In order to draw the hot-blooded Jonathan into battle on the plain, Apollonius first led his infantry toward the walls of Joppa, leaving a thousand horse behind in ambush. Then, as though reluctant to give battle, Apollonius withdrew his infantry. Sure enough, the ruse worked. The impetuous Jonathan came charging forward and followed Apollonius toward Ashdod. But once the Jews were fully committed to battle on the plain, Apollonius turned and attacked them.

It was a trick Jonathan had used himself, which makes it all the more surprising that he was caught by it—if indeed he were. For when Jonathan discovered the thousand horse at his rear, he at once formed a square. Command of the reserves he gave to his brother Simon while he himself took command of the defensive square. This stood fast with Jonathan, the men protected behind a solid wall of heavy shields locked together in the Roman fashion. The horses would not break through and the spears thrown by the horsemen were turned aside. When the enemy cavalry were out of spears and exhausted, Jonathan ordered Simon to charge them on the flank with his mobile reserves. The enemy infantry broke and fled and in the uproar the horses stampeded and scattered in wild confusion.

Jonathan pursued the enemy to the very gates of Ashdod then took the city on the first assault and burned it. He also burned the temple of Dagon with all the refugees inside. The total of the dead was reported to be eight thousand.

Moving southward Jonathan was welcomed at Ashkelon and, feeling secure in the south, he returned to Jerusalem, enriched and better armed than before. Alexander now hailed the victorious Jonathan as his friend and blithely repudiated Apollonius' whole campaign as not having had his sanction.

At this point the Egyptian Pharaoh, Ptolemy VI, called Philometor and regarded as the best of the Ptolemys, decided to march to the aid of his son-in-law Alexander in his struggle against the young Seleucid Demetrius II. Jonathan marched to meet him at Joppa in friendship.

But on reaching Ptolemais on the coast, the Ptolemy Philometor was surprised to discover he was the intended victim of a plot planned by Alexander, who was his son-in-law through marriage with his daughter Cleopatra. Philometor moved quickly. Instead of attacking Demetrius he made an alliance with him, and attacked Alexander instead. Taking Cleopatra prisoner, Philometor transferred his daughter's affections to Demetrius so that his new ally also became his new son-in-law. This expedient reversal gives some idea of the instability and confusion of the period.

Caught at last in one of the bewildering successions of intrigues, Jonathan was destroyed and his brother Simon took his place but did not long outlive him. It was the end of the four warrior brothers but not of the dynasty. Simon's son, John Hyrcanus, escaped capture and was welcomed into Jerusalem by its citizens, who made him high priest to succeed his father.

This remarkable family of military and administrative geniuses, aggressive, brave, vigorous, dedicated, resourceful, had for a long generation held at bay the Seleucid dynastic power and managed to do so with the merest pittance of money and a few men based in a tiny province. To accomplish so much, given only a small fraction of the territory, wealth, and manpower of their opponents, was one of the apparently miraculous phenomena of a people with a long tradition of doing the impossible. The Maccabees' exploits are among the most amazing in military history. The Lord God of Hosts apparently was with them.

After the death of Simon in 134 B.C., Judaea was torn asunder by the bitter hatreds of civil war. The seeds had been planted during the period of the Maccabees, when something in the nature of what we might call political parties arose in Judaea. In an amphictyony they were, of course, of a religious as well as of an economic and political nature.

The Sadducees, probably so-called because they claimed to be descended from Zadok, the head of the high priestly family in the time of David and Saul, were a clique of educated, wealthy men, nobles, and priests. Like most of their kind through the ages, they were conservative. Concerning the Jewish law this meant adhering to what was customary and resisting change. They repudiated all innovations and embellishments of the old laws and the old ways. They were hostile and suspicious of the oral tradition that was building up and winning acceptance as an unwritten Torah. They were in such a secure position economically that it was easy for them to endorse the Stoic doctrine of predestination.

In the Jewish Sanhedrin, which was a sort of combination legislature and supreme court, the Sadducees formed the majority. Because of conservatism and solidarity, they were on good terms with Rome but because they collected the tithes and operated the Temple, selling perfect beasts for the sacrifice and disposing of the meat afterward to the populace at a price, they were not popular. They responded by holding aloof. Yet, while dominating the Temple policies and ritual, they were also active as the money-changers and had general charge of the management and business of the Temple, which constantly brought them into dealings with the Hellenistic Gentiles. This tended to modify their exclusiveness and strict social adherence to the Mosaic law and brought them into closer touch with the practices and behavior of the surrounding culture. So, paradoxically, it was the Sadducees who were most likely to take up the prevailing Greek ways.

The Pharisees, on the other hand—the very word means "the separated ones"—were a minority group. There were only about six thousand of them, although several were members of the Sanhedrin. They considered themselves successors of Ezra and from their opponents' point of view they were newcomers. The first time we hear of them historically is during the time of John Hyrcanus though they were a sect before then. While they kept a scrupulous observance of the law—being in this respect successors to the Hasidim who, in 168 B.C., during the attack by Antiochus Epiphanes had chosen to die rather than fight on the Sabbath—they taught the oral law and added the Prophets and the Writings to the Torah.

The Pharisees were teachers and therefore were close to community life and with considerable influence over the people. They were the experts in Talmudic and Orthodox Judaism. They believed in God's guiding providence but they also believed in man's free will. Circulating among the people as they did, something of the Hellenistic philosophy rubbed off on them but outward compliance with Hellenistic social life was not possible for the strictest of them. They were pacifists, but they supported Jonathan and Simon against John Hyrcanus in the civil war. Liberal and progressive in thought, they endorsed the new feasts and festivals like the Feast of Lights and they actively proselytized for converts to Judaism. In fact, they preserved Judaism after the Temple was destroyed by Titus in A.D. 70 and the Sadducees no longer had any function.

A third group could hardly be called political although they were not without influence. These were the Essenes, a sort of monastic order of about four thousand religious men, and in rare cases their wives, who withdrew from the confusion and treachery of the bloody turmoil about them to devote themselves to study and prayer. They copied the books of wisdom and prophecy and the psalms which have come to light only recently as the Dead Sea Scrolls. Their community at Qumran on the heights northeast of Jerusalem overlooking the Dead Sea was well organized and disciplined. They lived a communal life so far as property and food were concerned and, more than any other group, dedicated themselves to a life of righteousness. They did not actively participate in the struggles for power that tore Judaea and Syria to pieces in their time but looked for a Messiah to deliver the Jews out of their affliction.

If the conflicts, alignments, and realignments in the last chapter seemed to verge on the bewildering, they were as simple as McGuffey's *First Reader* compared to what came afterward, and we may be excused for sparing ourselves a blow-by-blow account of such remote goings-on, and for taking the large view which excludes any focus on detail for its own sake.

John Hyrcanus was ambitious to restore Judaea to its former boundaries and glory, so the thirty years of his rule was not peaceful though he managed to remain politically independent. At first he was identified with the Pharisees but, quarreling with them, he went over to the opposition and threw in with the Sadducees. After his death in 104 B.C., his son Aristobulus took the title of king, and reigned for a year. His younger brother, Alexander Jannaeus, succeeded him and reigned until 76 B.C. In his time the Jews fought bitterly among themselves; probably the only thing that saved them from annihilation was that the Syrians were even less able to unite against them. These internecine brawls seem all the more suicidal when we recall that the aggressive Mithridates VI Eupator was king of Parthia at the time, while the Romans were subjugating one Hellenic city-state after another.

The Jewish factions became so embittered against one another that one faction even called in the hated sons of Edom to help besiege Jerusalem. As they had done many times before, the children of Israel quarreled when they should have been united in preparation against a common foe. There was no prophet now to warn them—as though that mattered, for when had they listened to their prophets? When do we? And it is ironic to think that their man-made quarrels were caused by zealous factional devotion to the worship of Yahweh. Yet even had they looked about them and seen what was going on in the world beyond their borders, it would have been too late, for Rome was in Damascus and Judaea was considered a tributary state. Her political freedom was at an end.

XX

THE ULTIMATE VICTORY

INTO DIVIDED PALESTINE came the Romans led by Pompey, determined to make Judaea a Roman province. Advancing on Jerusalem, he found the city very strongly fortified on every side though it was weakest on the north where the ground was higher outside the walls. A dry moat two hundred and fifty feet wide and sixty feet deep protected the walls on three sides of the city. The Temple, where the treasure was stored, was not only entirely within the walls of the city but was protected by walls of its own. The Temple grounds were on a raised plateau, connected with the city only by a single bridge across a deep ravine.

Pompey sent part of his army to demand entrance through the gates, whereupon one faction of the divided inhabitants admitted him to the city and to the palace of the Hasmonaeans which was near the bridge to the Temple enclosure. But the bridge had been destroyed.

Having won through the outer defenses, Pompey encamped facing the Temple on the north side. He patiently began filling in the dry moat while fetching his great siege engines from Tyre. As he daily advanced closer to the huge walls, the defending Jews helped him in a curious manner. Though they were allowed to *defend* themselves on the Sabbath, they were forbidden to take aggressive action. As soon as Pompey understood this peculiarity of their religious law, he simply waited until the Sabbath and during that day worked rapidly to fill the moat and advance his machinery and battering rams without being disturbed by any flight of arrows or stones hurled from the walls. Meanwhile sacrifices to Yahweh were performed daily in the Temple, even though great boulders came crashing through the roof.

At last the Temple was stormed. The ensuing slaughter was horrendous not only because the Romans were angry at the long and costly siege and cut down every Jew in sight, but also because the Jews of one faction set upon Jews of another faction, Pharisees against Sadducees. Altogether twelve thousand Jews died in exchange for a handful of Romans.

Entering the mysterious and forbidden inner Temple of Yahweh, Pompey, all curiosity, went into the Holy of Holies which was permitted only to the high priest himself on rare occasions. To his amazement he saw no idol or effigy. The seraphim throne was to all appearance empty. But the golden table, the holy silver candlestick, the pouring vessels of gold, the great store of rare spices, and a treasure of two thousand talents, Pompey left as he found them. He ordered the Temple cleansed of debris and commanded sacrifices to be brought in. Hyrcanus II was installed as high priest and ethnarch, which means "leader of the people," and Judaea was made a province under the Roman governor of Syria.

So the end result of the long, bitter struggle was that in 64 B.C. the Jews lost the political freedom they had long enjoyed under the Maccabees and lost much of the area those great military leaders had subjected.

A new dynasty that loomed large in the pages of the New Testament was founded at this time when in 55 B.C. Antipater Idumaea, the son of Antipater Antipas, became virtual ruler of all Palestine under the Romans. He was governor of Idumaea, succeeding his father who had been appointed by Alexander Jannaeus, a Maccabee. Both Antipater and his wife were Edomites, traditional enemies of the Israelites; they had two sons Phasael and Herod and a daughter Salome, a great-aunt of the notorious Salome mentioned by Luke in his Gospel.

Rome was torn apart when C. Julius Caesar defiantly crossed the Rubicon at the end of 50 B.C. The civil war between Pompey and his challenger ended when Pompey was defeated at Pharsalia in 48 B.C. He died soon after, assassinated in Egypt, and in 44 B.C. Caesar himself was assassinated by Brutus, Cassius, and a conspiracy of senators who, in their turn, were destroyed by the force of Marcus Antonius and Octavian—better known today as Mark Antony and Augustus.

Antony was appointed to rule over all the east as consul, and under him Herod the Great, son of Antipater, became tetrarch and later king of Judaea. This was the Herod referred to in the beginning of the Gospels according to St. Matthew and St. Luke.

In his amatory dalliance with Cleopatra, the Ptolemy queen of Egypt, Antony found life was not all love and kisses, for Cleopatra was an avaricious woman. She coaxed him into giving her Syria and tried to entice Judaea and Arabia from him; however, at that point he curbed his eagerness to please her, out of fear of his severely business-like colleague in Rome.

169

Cautious politician that he was, Herod paid Cleopatra tactful attention and on one occasion escorted her through Judaea and Jerusalem. Although Herod was a valuable friend of Rome, the Jews bitterly resented having an Edomite rule over them. They preferred to be governed by their own high priest of the Temple of Yahweh and to live in political freedom, subject only to their own Mosaic laws and their own representative governing body, the Sanhedrin. The Romans, tolerant of their worship and their laws, could not understand why the Jews were not tolerant in their turn. To Romans, the Jews seemed stiff-necked and bigoted.

Nevertheless, Jerusalem would have none of the Roman tetrarch Herod and rebelled against him. Herod based his army of Roman mercenaries on Jericho and laid siege to Jerusalem intending to attack the walls as Pompey had done, on the north side near the Temple. He prepared the siege machinery and "cut down the trees that were around about the city" as Josephus tells us.

The stubbornness of the resistance so infuriated the Romans that when they finally succeeded in taking the walls and had to fight from house to house to win the city, they vented their frustration in a fury of killing, old and young, women and babes, in a horror of blood. This battle for Jerusalem ended just twenty-seven years after Pompey's entrance into the city in the same way and on the same day, though this time with much greater slaughter.

The reign of Herod the Great, 37 B.C. to 4 B.C. was a reign of comparative peace, not merely because he was under the armed thumb of Rome, but because he had systematically killed off all the partisans of his late rival and even all those members of his own family who might conceivably have taken advantage of tax discontents to incite or lead a rebellion against him.

Herod was a great builder. Many structures and cities still bear the names he gave them. Samaria he handsomely rebuilt in the Greek manner renaming it Sebaste in honor of Augustus because

Sebaste means august one in Greek. Strato's Tower he turned into the superb marble-coated and colonnaded city of Caesaraea, also named for Caesar Augustus.

Herod was setting the scene for the New Testament. He entirely changed the appearance of Jerusalem with baths, amphitheater and hippodrome; it began to look like any other Hellenistic city. He built for himself a sumptuous palace in the northwest angle of the walls at the highest point of terrain near the Jaffa Gate, defended by three huge towers named after his brother Phasael, his wife Mariamne, and his friend Hippicus. To the north of the Temple enclosure and overlooking it, he raised a great fortified tower on the site of the old citadel that had been leveled by the Maccabees, and named it the Antonia Tower after his friend Mark Antony.

To pay for some of these lavish works, Herod opened David's tomb and helped himself to many precious vessels and materials, but when he tried to penetrate into the chamber where David and Solomon were buried, his torch ignited a gaseous substance that burst into a flash of flame and scared the grave-robber almost out of his wits, as a votive stone soon testified.

Noticing the relatively shabby appearance of the old Temple which had been built in the hard days after the return from Babylon, Herod at his own expense built one larger and even more magnificent than that built by Solomon in all his glory, using only the finest materials and most exquisite workmanship. Though the amphictyony had fallen on thin days, their shrine was enhanced in splendor, and yet in the doing of all this the Temple ceremonial was not interrupted by so much as one observance. This was, it seems, rather understanding in a king of the Jews who was not himself a Jew. The descendants of Israel were to know worse.

The work on the new Temple went on for a long time. The sanctuary was finished in a year and a half, but work on the cloisters and other parts of the structure continued for years. It was not completed by the time Jesus of Nazareth preached there; indeed, it was not finished until only a few years before it was once more, and perhaps finally, destroyed.

As well as giving the Jews a Temple that could hold its own for glory among the pagan temples in the Grecian style, Herod also respected their faith and laws. For instance, he did not place the usual emperor-statue in the Temple and avoided embellishing coins with portraits of himself or others.

Toward the end of his life Herod became suspicious and cruel, perhaps from bad health and pain. In any case, tormented by endless intrigues, charges and countercharges, he caused the death of three of his own sons. He had already killed his first wife, Mariamne. Exceeding his authority by making war against the Nabataeans as though he were an independent king, he drew down upon himself the displeasure of Augustus. The end of his life in 4 B.C. saw the breakdown of his character into a creature mean, arrogant, and cruel. But in his last year, a new star shone over Bethlehem and Jesus of Nazareth was born.

After the death of Herod, one of his sons, the harsh Archelaus, was appointed ethnarch of Judaea, Samaria, and Idumaea by the Emperor Augustus. Another son, the milder Herod Antipas, became tetrarch of Galilee and Peraea. It would have taken much better men than they were to acquit themselves well in the duty of extorting the last shekel out of the Jewish people for Rome.

In addition to the tremendous expense of their father's building program, which ground down the people whose sweat had to provide the money, the sons had the burden of imposing heavy taxes under the harsh demands of Rome, which was building a costly empire. The unrest was signalized shortly after the death of Herod the Builder when Sabrinus, the avaricious tax inspector of the emperor, drove the oppressed people of Judaea to a desperate fury of resentment against the imperium when he tried to rob both king and Temple. Jerusalem was in an uproar. To restore order, Varus, the legate of Syria, used a mailed fist against the bare flailing hands of the protesting people and, after two thousand rebellious Jews had been crucified, there was for a while outward quiet.

But, on complaint of the people to the emperor against his bad government, it was not long before Archelaus was removed as ethnarch and banished to Gaul. His brother, Herod Antipas (mentioned in the Gospels of Matthew, Mark, and Luke), now succeeded to his authority and territory more by common consent than by official action, for no one was specifically appointed to take the title of ethnarch.

As a matter of fact, the territory included in the jurisdiction of both Archelaus and Herod Antipas was presided over by a Roman procurator who was expected to live in Caesaraea and go to Jerusalem only during the festivals, when he might be in residence in Herod's palace with troops to keep order. This procurator was subordinate to the Roman legate of Syria. He had at his disposal only mercenary troops, for the legate commanded the Roman legion. One mark of the procurator's authority over the Jews was that he could appoint and dismiss the high priest at pleasure. Inasmuch as he was not a Jew, this was another cause of constant irritation.

In A.D. 26 a new procurator was sent out from Rome to govern Judaea, Samaria, and Idumaea. He was the son of a freedman and of equestrian rank who had been raised in the household of the Emperor Tiberius, successor to Augustus. His name was Pontius Pilate.

This man was a peculiar mixture of good and bad traits who tried to govern wisely and improve conditions in the territory under his authority but one of his principal failings was that he never could understand the peculiarities of the Jews. When he tried to be firm, he succeeded only in appearing unreasonable, arbitrary, unco-operative, and cruel. At best he irritated them.

When Pilate moved from Caesaraea to Jerusalem he brought

his mercenaries with him to take up winter quarters there, the city being a hotbed of trouble between factions both religious and political. His predecessors had customarily respected the religious scruples of the Jews against any graven image appearing in their holy city by leaving the eagles and standards bearing the picture of Caesar behind in Caesaraea, but for some reason of bravado, Pilate did not honor this custom. He brought the eagles and portraits with him and displayed these ensigns of Rome in full view in public places, having smuggled them into the city at night, which indicates he knew he was doing something that might cause a disturbance.

Soon after daylight the mob began to gather, crying out against the desecration. They assembled every day, bringing the business of the city to a standstill. On the sixth day, Pilate mounted his judgment seat in the public square, his troops concealed and ready behind him. When the mob pressed in upon him with an uproar of petitioning, he signaled the troops to surround them and ordered them to disperse.

This the mob refused to do, prostrating themselves on the ground and baring their necks, crying they would rather die than see their revered, ancient laws broken. Pilate, impressed by their sincerity and willingness to sacrifice themselves, drew back from the slaughter he would be held accountable for if he tried to uphold his foolish violation of their religious law. He gave in and ordered the offending standards to be carried back to Caesaraea.

When it came to the main business of being a procurator, which was to see that his province was governed in a way to make it profitable to Rome, to which end the Roman peace was a necessary instrument, Pilate was as wise and able an administrator as most of his contemporaries. Realizing that Jerusalem, like Rome, was not a productive community but a parasitic seat of government only, he saw the same conditions prevailing there as in Rome —great overcrowding, congestion, and consequent restless discontent. In Jerusalem water was always a serious problem, especially during the festivals when multitudes gathered in and around the city. So Pilate constructed a series of storage reservoirs and aqueducts to bring more water into the city. Since it was for the benefit of the whole Jewish population and the Temple of Yahweh, he thought it proper to use the Temple money to pay for it.

But the people thought otherwise. To use the sacred funds without permission of the high priest seemed sacrilegious to them; before long a crowd gathered and began to abuse Pilate.

Pilate had some reason to feel indignant at this ingratitude and his resentment took the usual form of violence. Unable to disperse the unruly mob, he disguised some of his troops as civilians and sent them through the crowd. Then at a signal they began to beat the rioters with clubs quite indiscriminately, beating many of them to death. The crowd ran away, but the feud between the populace and Rome was only intensified by this event.

Perhaps acting from pique at the behavior of the Jewish people whom he quite failed to understand, much less sympathize with, Pilate caused the blood of some executed Galileans to be mingled with the blood of the sacrifices. The roar of indignation that went up at this sacrilege seemed to him amazingly out of all proportion.

When Jesus (in Hebrew Yeshua, a later form of Joshua) of Nazareth entered Jerusalem six days before Passover, probably in the year A.D. 30, riding on a white ass, a symbol of royalty since the days before David, the city was seething with unrest and suppressed excitement. Jews were gathering for the festival from all over the known world. Simon and his sons, for instance, had come from far away Cyrene in Africa. The city was overflowing and families were encamped on the hills around the capital.

Pontius Pilate was in residence in the Antonia Citadel overlooking the crowded Temple enclosure. King Herod was in residence in his father's palace across the city. The high priest and his family occupied the palace of the Hasmonaeans which was conveniently located near the bridge to the Temple, at the other end of which was the chamber of the Sanhedrin.

When Jesus began preaching in the outer courts of the Temple, an audience was ready-made at any hour. Pilgrims were buying creatures for the sacrifice to God—white doves for the poor, lambs and oxen for those who could afford them.

The purchase money was of every kind minted by all the nations of the world, and had to be exchanged into currency especially minted by the Temple, a currency that would contain no graven image, no portrait of man or beast. The business of changing the currencies was highly profitable for the money-changers who were the Sadducees.

The tremendous success of Jesus's preaching and the ecstatic response from the crowds increased from hour to hour as word of him spread among the multitudes. Here was a leader indeed, a Messiah promised them by the prophets Micah and Isaiah, who would lead them out of their afflictions and deliver them from their enemies, the heavy-handed tax collectors of Rome.

Envious and suspicious of his popularity, the Sadducees began to heckle Jesus. He was telling the populace that the sacrifice most acceptable to God was a contrite heart. This threatened to interfere with their lucrative business and curtail their fabulous wealth. Besides this, Jesus was a Pharisee. It was easy to hear from his own lips that he could not possibly be a Sadducee.

The Pharisees also heckled Jesus, though they had no more success than their opponents. They refused to accept him as one of their faction. Was he not preaching that to fear God and love your neighbor was all the law and the prophets? The rest is only illustration, he might have added in the words of the great Gamaliel and Hillel before him. If this were all, what would become of the teaching profession of the Pharisees? But worse than that, he sat down to eat with publicans and sinners and was careless of the prescribed rituals which the Pharisees observed in meticulous detail. Jesus was a man without a party.

Seeking to entrap Jesus, the priests showed him a Roman coin and asked him to whom it belonged. When he asked whose was the face and inscription thereon, they eagerly replied, "Caesar's." "Render to Caesar the things that are Caesar's," he replied, "and to God the things that are God's."

In a fury of indignation he threw over the high-piled tables of the money-changers who were doing business in the Temple arcades, and as the currency of the nations of the world rolled clattering over the pavement, he seized a whip from one of the Temple police and beat the priestly clerks, crying, "My house is the house of prayer: but ye have made it a den of thieves."

The people were in a transport of delight and worship. But the new, secret sect of fanatical nationalists called Zealots were dismayed. One of their leaders, the bandit Jesus Barabbas, had been arrested, thrown into prison and sentenced to be crucified. Was this unarmed, peaceful man without money, weapons, or troops going to spoil their plans? They too were implacably opposed to Jesus of Nazareth.

All this and much more Jesus understood. He heard it, he felt it, he knew it. Fully realizing that the restless, bitter foment working underground would inevitably break out in open rebellion against Rome, Jesus pointed to the magnificent towering structure of the Temple of huge hewn stones that was now at last almost completed, and scandalized his disciples by telling them the day was not far off when "There shall not be left here one stone upon another, that shall not be thrown down" (Matt. 24:2).

All the leaders of the various factions knew the pressure would burst its bounds at any moment. The Zealots, the followers of Barabbas, were working for it with fanatical fury under cover. So were the Sadducees and the high priest Caiaphas. The Pharisees were divided, not organized for concerted action. Pilate was in a torment of worry for fear there would be great bloodshed and that his political career, already under a cloud in Rome for the disturbances and chronic unrest in his province, would be ruined. To avert open rebellion, the situation would have to be handled and handled quickly. But how?

The Sadducees moved first. After the incident of the money-changers there was no time to lose. Jesus spoke like one having authority. From whom? They looked slantingly at one another, not daring to answer their own question.

To bring down Jesus from the pedestal where the people had put him, they must act not only quickly but in secret. They broke many of their own laws in order to do this.

Bribing one of his followers to point him out to the Temple police sent to arrest him, he was discovered at night almost alone in the Garden of Gethsemane, just across the Kidron opposite the Temple grounds. As the leader of the police, a kinsman of the high priest, laid his hand on Jesus, the Apostle Simon called Peter drew a sword and cut off his ear, thus making the man ineligible to serve in the Temple. Small wonder Peter was in mortal terror of being identified thereafter. Luke, the physician, says Jesus "healed" the ear, but Matthew and Mark say nothing about healing, though they both report the incident.

This was the only blow struck in what some consider the most decisive battle of the Bible. Jesus forbade any further bloodshed and gave himself up.

Jesus was hurried before the Sanhedrin, not sitting in full session but with a quorum of Sadducees only, present. By moving so swiftly, and at night, the high priest was able to pretend there was no time to notify such leading influential Pharisees as Nicodemus and Joseph of Arimathaea, a rich merchant with many powerful friends among the Romans, including Pilate himself.

The Sadducees broke their own law when they tried a man by night; they broke another when they condemned him on the same day they tried him.

Taking Jesus before Pilate in the middle of the night, the Sadducees did their best to make out a case that he was treasonable to Rome. Pilate was puzzled. He could find no harm in Jesus from the Roman point of view. When he heard Jesus was from Galilee, Pilate was suddenly relieved and slyly amused. Herod was tetrarch of Galilee and in residence. He would send Jesus to Herod for judgment as a rival king of the Jews and thus have his little joke. At the same time he would be rid of the responsibility of a decision concerning the fate of Jesus.

But the plan did not work. Herod only laughed. He could not imagine the son of a carpenter in a farming community, like Galilee, a mere itinerant preacher, as king of anything. He mocked Jesus and sent him back to Pilate, requesting only that Jesus be labeled as one who *called* himself King of the Jews and not "King of the Jews."

Pilate was galled and irritated to find the problem back on his doorstep and refused to edit his words but continued sarcastically to refer to Jesus as King of the Jews.

Meanwhile, busy all the night, the Sadducees had sent out their special police to assemble a mob from among the faction favorable to them. Early in the morning, shortly after cock-crow, Pilate was faced again with his dilemma, the crowd pressing in around his residence, demanding the punishment of the imposter Jesus and the freedom of their warlike leader Barabbas.

Pilate questioned Jesus again. There was, of course, a language barrier; Jesus spoke Aramaic and Koine, Pilate spoke Latin. They understood few words between them, but those few were fruitful with meaning. Even with many words in common, they might not have said more. "To this end was I born, and for this cause came I into the world," said Jesus, in answer to a question from Pilate, "that I should bear witness unto the truth."

"What is truth?" asked Pilate, perhaps gesturing toward the violent differences of opinions in the mob before them. Jesus knew the futility of words at this stage of events and said nothing more.

The crowd was growing wild and dangerous. Murderous. "Crucify him!" they yelled. "And give us Barabbas!" For it had been the custom for the governor to free a political prisoner at the request of the people on a festival day.

But Pilate from his judgment seat said, "I have examined him before you and have found no fault in this man touching those things whereof you accuse him; no nor yet Herod; for I sent you to him; and, lo, nothing worthy of death is done unto him."

"Crucify him," yelled the hysterical mob.

It was best, thought Pilate, to give in to, to humor the furious people. By this means only could he avoid having them take the law into their own hands. So, to keep the Roman peace, he let them have their way, futilely trying to purge himself of any responsibility for the result of his surrender by washing his hands of the whole affair before their glittering eyes.

When Jesus from the cross cried out the opening words of the Twenty-second Psalm which recounts from ancient days the prophecy of his Messianic mission and his Passion—the Psalm that begins with the words "My God, my God, why hast thou forsaken me?"—his voice failed him from the great torment he was in. Even at the end, the prophecy "not a bone of him shall be broken" was fulfilled, for against custom he was pierced in the side by a compassionate centurion instead of having his legs broken like others crucified.

A generation later, in A.D. 66, while Paul's letters were being circulated and read in new churches, the political unrest and religious ferment that had pervaded the environment of the ministry of Jesus finally erupted into open, armed rebellion. It took the determined might of Rome, led by Vespasian and Titus, nearly four years to reconquer the Jews. At the end, in A.D. 70, Jerusalem was taken, the treasure of the Temple was carried away to Rome, and the Temple and the walls were pulled down until, as Jesus had prophesied, "not one stone" remained standing on another. Grass grew in the streets and the land became a desert. The people scattered. It would be another day in a later time with another Exodus, before the children of Israel would once again come home.

The decisive victory of Jesus on Calvary seemed at first like a defeat. The consequences of it were not at once apparent, neither to his followers, nor even to the wretched Pilate. But the sacrifice of Jesus on the cross was only a beginning, for although the Christian centuries have witnessed many cruel wars and bitter battles, both in Palestine and throughout Christendom, the Lord God moves in a way altogether mysterious and those who have faith believe with the prophet Micah that men of peace will win the ultimate victory.

INDEX

Index

Index

Index